Home Office Research Study 273

Accrediting Offender Programmes: A process-based evaluation of the Joint Prison/Probation Services Accreditation Panel

Sue Rex, Roxanne Lieb, Anthony Bottoms and Louise Wilson
Institute of Criminology, University of Cambridge

The views expressed in this report are those of the authors, not necessarily those of the Home Office (nor do they reflect Government policy).

Home Office Research, Development and Statistics Directorate
November 2003

Home Office Research Studies

The Home Office Research Studies are reports on research undertaken by or on behalf of the Home Office. They cover the range of subjects for which the Home Secretary has responsibility. Other publications produced by the Research, Development and Statistics Directorate include Findings, Statistical Bulletins and Statistical Papers.

The Research, Development and Statistics Directorate

RDS is part of the Home Office. The Home Office's purpose is to build a safe, just and tolerant society in which the rights and responsibilities of individuals, families and communities are properly balanced and the protection and security of the public are maintained.

RDS is also part of National Statistics (NS). One of the aims of NS is to inform Parliament and the citizen about the state of the nation and provide a window on the work and performance of government, allowing the impact of government policies and actions to be assessed.

Therefore –

Research Development and Statistics Directorate exists to improve policy making, decision taking and practice in support of the Home Office purpose and aims, to provide the public and Parliament with information necessary for informed debate and to publish information for future use.

First published 2003

Application for reproduction should be made to the Communications and Development Unit, Room 201, Home Office, 50 Queen Anne's Gate, London SW1H 9AT.

© Crown copyright 2003   ISBN 1 84473 127.8

ISSN 0072 6435

Foreword

The Joint Prison/Probation Service Accreditation Panel (now called the Correctional Services Accreditation Panel) was established by the Home Secretary in July 1999 as part of the Government's Crime Reduction Programme. Its task is to ensure that treatment programmes which offenders undergo to reduce the likelihood of their re-offending are of high quality and are effective. This work is crucial to the modernisation of the Probation Service and to improving the effectiveness of prisons.

This report presents findings from an evaluation of the effectiveness of Correctional Services Accreditation Panel between December 2001 and September 2002. The purpose of the evaluation was to examine the performance of the Panels central functions of accrediting offender treatment programmes and monitoring their post-accreditation delivery.

The evaluation found that the Panel functioned well between December 2001 and September 2002 but makes a number of recommendations on how to improve the accreditation process and the workings of the Panel. Most recommendations were met when a new panel was appointed prior to March 2003.

Chloë Chitty
Programme Director
Offending and Criminal Justice (What Works)

Acknowledgments

There are many people working in different organisations without whose assistance this study would not have been possible. We are grateful to those working in the Home Office, Probation and Prison Services, the Courts Service and the Magistrates' Association, and to members of the Judiciary and the Magistracy, who helped us to arrange or contributed to our fieldwork. We are also grateful to the chairman of the Joint Accreditation Panel, Sir Duncan Nichol, and to all Panel members for giving so freely of their time to talk to us, and for allowing us to observe Panel meetings. Thanks go too to our University-based colleagues who contributed to our academic seminar or otherwise provided advice and material, especially to Ellie Scrivens for her particular generosity. We also received useful information from those working with the Canadian and Scottish Accreditation Panels.

Particular thanks go to Dr Gareth Hughes, Head of Psychological Services at Kneesworth House Hospital and Research Fellow at the Institute, for his specialist psychology advice.

We also received a great deal of help from Julian Norris, Mark May and John Lympany of the Panel Secretariat, and from Robin Elliot and Laura Blakeborough in the Research Development and Statistics Directorate, for which we are most grateful.

Sue Rex
Roxanne Lieb
Anthony Bottoms
Louise Wilson

Contents

Summary

This report presents findings on a process-based evaluation of the effectiveness of the Joint Prison/Probation Services Accreditation Panel (JAP) (now the Correctional Services Accreditation Panel (CSAP)), in the performance of its central function of accrediting offender programmes and their delivery.

Introduction (Chapter 1)

The Panel performs an important function in assisting the Prison and Probation Services to achieve their aim of using What Works principles to reduce re-offending through the development and implementation of high quality offender programmes accredited by the Panel. It was set up by the Home Office and Prison Service as part of the Government's Crime Reduction Programme, with appointments to the Panel made in July 1999.

The evaluation was conducted against a context of change in the remit and business of the Panel. As well as a new name, Ministers have approved new terms of reference representing largely a natural evolution of the Panel's remit. An important change to the terms of reference marks a move into 'integrated systems', covering approaches to assessment, referral, case management and throughcare. Accordingly, a new set of integrated systems criteria – as well as revised programme accreditation criteria – were produced for use by the Panel at its meeting in September 2002. Another major development is the recruitment of a new Panel under the continuing chairmanship of Sir Duncan Nichol.

Research brief and methodology (Chapter 2)

The evaluation took place between December 2001 and September 2002. It draws on 394 questionnaires completed by stakeholders, and interviews with 106 individuals, as well as observation and documentary analysis, as follows:

- Observation of the JAP meeting in February/March 2002 and the Drugs Sub Panel in May 2002, plus interviews with panel members.

- 25 interviews with key policy administrators in the Prison and Probation Services, and with implementation managers and programme developers.

- An academic seminar with nine University-based researchers and evaluators, hosted by RDS.

- 167 questionnaires completed by staff managing and delivering accredited programmes in six prison establishments and five probation areas (a response rate of 66%). Interviews with a representative cross section of 46 local staff. Efforts were made to obtain the views of ethnic minority programme staff.

- 50 questionnaires completed by personal officers working in the five prisons (a response rate of 20%). Questionnaires were also sent to probation PSR authors and case managers but too few were completed to justify analysis.

- 177 questionnaires completed by judges and magistrates sitting in the localities in which prison and probation views were sampled (a response rate of 46%), and interviews with eight senior sentencers.

- A review of literature relating to the accreditation of offender programmes in other jurisdictions and in other public sectors in the UK, and analysis of policy papers relating to JAP and to relevant activities in the Prison and Probation Services.

Very different response rates were received from the samples above and it cannot be determined whether the views of non-respondents would have differed from those who did respond, but it is reasonable to assume that the lower the response rate, the less representative respondents' views are likely to be. Caution is therefore required in interpreting some of the findings, particularly those relating to prison personal officers.

Role and organisation of the Panel (Chapter 3)

Panel membership: The clearest views to emerge from stakeholders were that JAP required more expertise in substance misuse programmes as well as a more ethnically diverse membership, both matters that recruitment for the new Panel has sought to address. It was also seen as important to preserve the academic strength and independence of the Panel, as well as the emphasis on maintaining high standards in programme accreditation. Indeed, the intention in appointing the new Panel was to restore the balance in favour of appointed members by reducing the permanent nominated – or ex officio – membership to just three individuals. Given the presence on the Panel of programme developers, one concern related to a possible indirect conflict of interest when the Panel was considering a programme in which a Panel member had an interest (even though, under existing rules, he or she is excluded from the relevant sub panel discussion of that programme).

Functioning of meetings: The general view from Panel members was that two five day meetings of the main Panel enabled them to balance other commitments with the need to get through JAP business, although they recognised the need for supplementary meetings of the Drug and Audit Sub Panels. Levels of satisfaction with the support provided by the JAP secretariat were high, and Panel members appreciated the quality of advice from the diversity advisor, and seconded experts on drugs misuse and community punishment.

Some specific suggestions to improve the continuity and functioning of the Panel emerged particularly from interviews with JAP members and programme developers:

- Intersperse plenary and sub panel meetings during the JAP week, to enable a sub panel to consider a specific issue and bring proposals to a plenary meeting.

- Arrange a meeting of sub panel chairs at some point during the week, to talk over common issues that have arisen at sub panel meetings.

- Appoint previewers (from Panel membership) of programme submissions to brief sub panel discussions.

- Set up a database to track submissions through the Panel, and provide sub panels with a digest of previous decisions and who contributed to them.

- Provide additional advice through research briefings to update panel members on recent literature relating to the range of programmes coming before them, and on ethical questions.

First recommendation: Introduce a clear distinction between full panel members, whether appointed or nominated, and other participants. Consider: only full members to have 'voting' rights; only full members to act as sub panel chairs; previewers or shepherds to be selected from full membership.

Second recommendation: Clarify/publicise the arrangements to prevent potential conflicts of interest when the Panel is considering a submission in which a member has an interest, or what might be construed as an interest. Consider requiring a panel member who has acted as consultant to a programme to withdraw from Panel membership for a period, to ensure that he or she does not attend the Panel week in which the programme is being considered.

Third recommendation: Improve JAP paperwork management and introduce clearer records of sub panel discussion and decisions. Consider setting up a database to track submissions through the Panel, and provide sub panels with a digest of previous decisions and who contributed to them.

Accrediting programmes (Chapter 4)

Progress of programmes: In just over two years, the panel has accredited 15 programmes in six meetings (including the meeting in February/March 2002). Six of these programmes are for sex offenders, five are general offending behaviour programmes, two programmes tackle aggression and violence, one addresses drink impaired driving and another substance misuse. The progress of these programmes towards accreditation has been as follows:

- seven programmes achieved accreditation at their first formal submission for that status (four following 'advice' from the Panel)

- seven programmes achieved accreditation at their second formal submission (four were separately submitted for advice at least once)

- one programme required three formal submissions before gaining accredited status (following initial advice from the Panel)

Accreditation process: Panel members emphasised what they saw as the collaborative constructive spirit in which they considered submissions for accreditation and advice. Programme developers shared this view of the Panel's approach to its work, but sometimes perceived a tendency for academic debate to overshadow the provision of practical 'What Works' advice. A point of common agreement was the need for high standards to maintain the credibility of accredited programmes, while at the same time taking care not to make accreditation a virtually insurmountable hurdle. Generally, local programme staff also rated JAP decisions fairly positively, with half seeing its decisions as good or very good, and viewed accredited programmes as effective and workable. In their experience of submitting programmes, some programme developers identified a need for more specific guidance about the Panel's requirements through pro-forma or examples of what had been found helpful in earlier submissions. They also expressed some frustration that panel members were not always fully familiar with written submission material, and stated a wish for fuller consultation with panel members about the Panel's requirements, perhaps in the context of site visits by panel members to see how a programme ran in practice. As gatekeepers, headquarters personnel in the Prison and Probation Services were seen as performing an important role in targeting the resources of the Panel in accordance with agency priorities, but were not always seen as effective in managing submissions and communicating Panel expectations to applicants.

Accreditation criteria: Panel members found the accreditation criteria operated as a flexible and workable tool, and endorsed the arrangements by which submissions were scored. They saw the new criteria as more accessible to applicants, as accommodating a broader range of programmes and as addressing diversity (meeting some of the reservations about a cognitive behavioural bias expressed by programme developers). Programme managers reported a fair amount of knowledge of the criteria (though 49% of tutors reported 'no' knowledge) and 79 per cent of programme staff agreed that the criteria 'set high standards that increase the likelihood of effectiveness'. Diversity emerged as an issue, with only a quarter of staff agreeing that the standards set by the criteria were applicable to all offenders and, over two-fifths believing that they failed to take account of the needs of some offenders.

Diversity: In interview, programme developers and evaluators and staff delivering programmes expressed doubts about whether the range of programmes accredited so far met the needs of ethnic minorities, female offenders and offenders with learning difficulties. JAP interviewees and programme developers both saw diversity as presenting a challenge with which the accreditation process had been slow to engage, although recent progress was noted. Views were divided on whether to include a specific diversity criterion, or whether the solution lay in careful monitoring of how diversity was addressed in the design and delivery of programmes.

Panel costs: The direct costs of the Panel remained reasonably stable over the period of its operation so far. Official expenditure in 2001/02, at just over £230,000, was slightly higher than in 2000/01 but included the costs of the evaluation (1999/2000 was not a full year of operation). Direct costs in 2001/02 totalled £371,376, including secretariat (£48,301), letter writers (£6,950) and commitments by ex-officio members or participants (£84,729). The costs of a Panel Day in 2001/02 were estimated at £14,248, covering the cost of the personnel listed above (slightly below £10,000 per day) plus accommodation. It costs between £25,000 to £30,000 to get a typical 'in-service' programme accredited by the Panel (involving two submissions).

Fourth recommendation: Provide clearer guidance on the structure of programme submissions and the contents of the different manuals. Consider introducing pro-forma manuals, or where this is inappropriate provide examples of material that has previously been found helpful. Consider how Panel feedback might make a clearer distinction between adjustments that are required before accreditation can be achieved as opposed to changes that are desirable.

Fifth recommendation: Appoint panel members as previewers of programme submissions to brief and guide sub panel discussion. Consider site visits by previewer(s) to liaise with programme developers about Panel requirements, and observe delivery of programme. Consider arrangements to ensure that the previewer does not commit the Panel to a particular decision, for example by not chairing the sub panel considering the submission.

Sixth recommendation: Consider submission of non-paper material, for example videos, presentations by programme developers or implementation managers, electronic format (CD roms).

Other contributions to 'What Works' (Chapter 5)

Cultural change: Overall, there was a clear endorsement by programme staff of the 'What Works' project to which JAP was contributing. The vast majority, including all managers and 70 per cent of tutors, had heard of JAP, usually through colleagues. Over 40 per cent of programme staff understood its role as about 'quality control', although actual knowledge of JAP's decisions was limited. Prison personal officers showed a high level of awareness of 'What Works' research, and saw themselves as reasonably informed about local programmes, although most had no knowledge of Panel decisions. In interview, some programme staff saw their information about the work of the Panel as inadequate and suggested that the following would be useful:

- an information pack for treatment managers to use with tutors or colleagues

- bulletins about research evidence for tutors to use with colleagues and offenders

- a HQs 'help line' for queries about programme material and delivery

- a 'news' section on NPD website, intranet; online reference manuals

- inputs at training events for treatment managers and tutors.

Sentencers' views: Sentencers saw themselves as reasonably well informed about programme effectiveness, about accredited programmes, and especially about programmes available locally. There was clearly an appetite for more information about effectiveness and programme content. This was seen as likely to enhance sentencers' confidence in community-based programmes for offenders. Suggestions included:

- loose-leaf booklet in the Retiring Room, regularly updated

- videos, bulletins, lunch time presentations

- direct contact with staff delivering programmes, and visits to programmes

- leaflet or summary of programme attached to PSRs

- e-mail summaries of new programme content

- information published in 'The Magistrate' or by HM Probation Inspectorate.

Curriculum development: Much of the Panel's contribution to curriculum development took the form of standard setting and advice and feedback to applicants for advice or accreditation. The piloting of new approaches was seen as the remit of the Prison and Probation Services. Panel members and programme developers clearly valued the opportunity for feedback and dialogue on submission.

Audit: The audit of programme delivery was carried out by Prison Service Headquarters and HM Inspectorate of Probation according to arrangements approved by the Panel. Some disquiet was expressed about the disparity of audit arrangements and the apparent application of tougher standards in probation than in prison audits, with implications for achievements of KPI targets. Progress was slow in meeting the Panel's wish to move towards a unified system of audit for both correctional services.

Seventh recommendation: In order to increase the Panel's visibility and the transparency of its decisions, there is a need for a strategic approach to communication between the Panel and staff in the correctional services on a range of issues. There is also a need to ensure that the Panel plays an appropriate role in informing sentencers about programme effectiveness. Consider the following mechanisms: intranet, internet and e-mail; information pack distributed to treatment managers; accessible booklets for sentencers regularly updated; panel members to visit programme sites, and contribute to conferences and training events; seminars with programme staff to debate important issues e.g. diversity, models of change for women, programme integrity, responsibility.

Eighth recommendation: Pending the introduction of a unified system of audit for the correctional services, a body outside the Prison Service Sentence Management Group should undertake the audit function.

Future directions (Chapter 6)

A number of structural issues pertain to the legitimacy of the Panel: its role in programme development, access to the Panel (gatekeeping), and oversight of audit arrangements. Overall, JAP appears to have performed well in establishing its legitimacy, but it might usefully review its practices in the light of the literature on procedural justice. Important areas of future development in the Panel's role include: contributing to curriculum development and effective programme implementation; reviewing accredited programmes in the light of research and practitioner feedback; and the accreditation of integrated systems. As it develops its collaboration with the Correctional Services, the Panel will wish to ensure that its role remains clearly delineated.

1.   Introduction

The research presented in this report was commissioned by the Research Development and Statistics Directorate (RDS) in the Home Office. Conducted between December 2001 and September 2002, its purpose was to conduct a process-based evaluation of the work of the Joint Accreditation Panel (JAP) in the performance of its central functions of accrediting offender treatment programmes and monitoring their post-accreditation delivery. Before describing the methodology for the research and reporting the findings, this chapter starts by reviewing the background to the Panel, and recent developments in its role.

Background to the Panel and the policy context

The Joint Accreditation Panel (full title, the Joint Prison/Probation Services Accreditation Panel) was set up in 1999 by the Home Office and the Prison Service as part of the Government's Crime Reduction Programme.[1] It replaced the Prison Service's earlier General and Sex Offender Treatment Programme Accreditation Panels, which had been established in 1996. Essentially, its role is first, to accredit offender treatment programmes against a set of criteria based on so-called "'What Works' principles" for the prison and probation services to use in reducing re-offending (the aim of the accreditation process being to produce a core curriculum of demonstrably effective programmes).[2] Secondly, it oversees the audit arrangements to monitor the delivery of such programmes after accreditation.

Appointments to the Panel were initially made (in accordance with the Code of Practice on Public Appointments) in July 1999, for a period of three years; and the Panel held its first meeting in November 1999. The Panel is chaired by Sir Duncan Nichol, formerly Chief Executive of the National Health Service, who was re-appointed for a further three years

---

1   The Panel's name was changed to the Correctional Services Accreditation Panel in late Summer 2002; however, the Panel is referred to throughout this report as the Joint Accreditation Panel (JAP) as this is the name by which it was known during the data collection.
2   In so doing, the Panel is contributing to the Home Office's 'What Works' Strategy, originally launched by the Home Office and HM Probation Inspectorate in 1998 as the Effective Practice Initiative, which has prioritised the reduction of re-offending amongst the aims of the correctional services. Effective practice, or 'What Works', is informed by a set of principles originally compiled by McGuire (1995), and promulgated by HM Probation Inspectorate in Underdown (1998).

(until May 2005) while this evaluation was being conducted. Membership of the Panel comprises two separate categories: 'appointed members', who are independent experts, and 'nominated members', who hold official positions connected to the prison and probation services. At the time of our evaluation, there were 12 appointed members and seven nominated members, and the Home Office was in the process of recruiting a new Panel (not finalised until after the research was completed). The terms of reference for the Panel and its composition as the evaluation started are set out in Appendix I, together with a summary of its accreditation criteria. The latter were revised following consideration at the February/March 2002 meeting of the Panel, as will be discussed later in this report.

According to its Second Report 2000-2001, the Panel regards its key task as enabling the prison and probation services to equip themselves with interventions that will reduce offending, and it sees insistence on high quality programmes as a necessary feature of that function. The Panel's work is supported by a secretariat comprising both Prison Service headquarters and National Probation Directorate staff, and it considers programmes largely sponsored for submission by Prison Service headquarters and the National Probation Directorate (who each act as 'gatekeepers' at the interface between the Panel and the field, as we shall describe more fully later). Private and non-profit making organisations can also submit programmes to the Panel (and sometimes do so without 'gatekeeping' by Prison HQ or the Probation Directorate), but such applications form only a small minority of the submissions considered by the Panel.

Constitutionally, the Panel is a non-departmental public body (NDPB) with an independent chair.[3] In practice, the Panel works very closely with its two linked agencies, and its activities are to a large extent shaped by the policy priorities of these two services. Specifically, the correctional services see it as their responsibility to decide how many offending programmes of what type they need, and they target their own resources, and influence the work of the Panel, accordingly. The prison service determines its priorities through its What Works Strategy Board, and the probation service through its What Works Clans.

The main business of the Panel is conducted at two separate week-long meetings of the whole Panel each year. During these weeks, the Panel occasionally meets in plenary session, and normally does so on the final (Friday) morning of the week. More often, it works through its formal Audit Sub Panel and Drugs Sub Panel (each with a fixed membership), as well as through less formal ad hoc 'sub panels' or working groups. In 2001/02, both the Audit and the Drugs Sub Panels convened additional meetings, separately from the main Panel meetings, in order to complete their respective workloads.

---

3   A non-departmental public body is a body established by Government, sometimes but not always under legislation, which is publicly funded but exists independently of any government department. Examples include the Youth Justice Board and Parole Board.

When making submissions for accreditation, programme developers are required to submit five manuals to the Panel. They are: the theory manual to set out the model of change; the programme manual to describe each session in the programme; the assessment and evaluation manual; the management manual; and the staff training manual. As well as being formally 'accredited', applications may be graded by the Panel as 'recognised' (where it is considered that specified changes can be achieved within 12 months to achieve accreditation); 'promising' (substantial further work is required, after which accreditation may be achieved); or 'no further review warranted' (the programme has little hope of being accredited).

As well as considering programmes for accreditation, an important part of the Panel's work is to provide preliminary advice to programmes before a formal accreditation application is made. These 'applications for advice' can be beneficial both to programme developers (because they are given an early indication of the Panel's view of the strengths and weaknesses of the programme) and to the Panel itself (because it enables the Panel to contribute substantially to programme development). According to the Panel's Second Report, this provision of advice has helped to produce positive results when programmes are later considered for accreditation.

The Panel's developing role

The research evaluation concentrated on the Panel's existing terms of reference in examining the work of the Panel, and its impact in the prison and probation services. However, the evaluation was undertaken against a context of change in the remit and business of the Joint Accreditation Panel, which it was necessary for the evaluation to take into account.

The most important change was the approval by Ministers of new terms of reference for JAP after its meeting in February/March 2002. Along with the new name, these substantially extend the business of the Panel. The paper proposing the new terms of reference noted that the changes would require the Panel to have a clearer, forward-looking view of its work and strategic role, matched to the resources allocated. Some of the changes were a natural evolution of the Panel's previous remit – these included taking a more proactive stance on curriculum development; ensuring that diversity is taken into account in accredited programmes; and adopting a higher profile in communicating with staff across the correctional services.

More fundamentally, the new terms of reference also require the Panel to assist in identifying training requirements common to several accredited programmes, to minimise unnecessary duplication; and to move to a wider assessment of the impact and effectiveness of programmes, taking account of audit and evaluation findings. Another new term of reference articulates the role of the Panel as an advisory body to the correctional services, providing an innovative perspective for change informed (but not bound) by close liaison with the services on issues such as operational impact, deliverability and cost. A further important – and radical – change to the terms of reference marks a move into 'integrated systems'.[4] Accordingly, a new set of integrated systems criteria – as well as revised programme accreditation criteria – was produced for use by the Panel at its meeting in September 2002 (after the research fieldwork was completed).

Following consultation, Ministers have decided not to expand the Panel's remit to programmes commissioned by the Youth Justice Board for the time being, although the change in its name to Correctional Services Accreditation Panel is indicative of a move towards a potentially broader approach.

As was recognised at the time these various developments were proposed, the changes have potential implications for the future composition of the Panel, which might need to call upon a wider spectrum of experience and expertise, for example as regards the integrated systems approach and in considering diversity issues.

Structure of the research report

The remainder of this report is structured as follows. The next chapter (Chapter 2) describes the research design and the sources of data upon which the report draws. Chapter 3 then discusses the composition of the Panel, and organisational matters related to how it conducts its business. Chapter 4 considers the Panel's main activity of accrediting programmes, as well as the costs incurred. Chapter 5 addresses other important aspects of the Panel's work in contributing to effective practice: namely, advising on curriculum development; advising on the audit of programmes; and contributing to a culture of effectiveness within the prison and probation services. Finally, Chapter 6 looks to the likely future development of the role of the Panel in the light of the recent decisions by Ministers (see above) and the findings presented in this report.

---

4   'Integrated systems' cover arrangements, such as assessment, referral and case management, intended to ensure that the conditions in which interventions are implemented support their effective delivery and provide appropriate aftercare. There is an analogy in the health setting, where the success of a patient's recovery from an operation will depend in part upon the adequacy of the arrangements for post-operative care and rehabilitation. One example in the criminal justice setting is the 'through the gate' proposals by the Social Exclusion Unit for a continuous model of case management spanning imprisonment and release into the community (Social Exclusion Unit, 2002).

2.   Research Brief and Methodology

Evaluation aims

As stated in the introduction to this report, the key aim of the research was to conduct a process-based evaluation of JAP in the performance of its central functions of accrediting programmes and monitoring their subsequent delivery. More specifically, the main research questions (as agreed with RDS, the research sponsors) were as follows:

1. Are the current composition and the working arrangements of the Panel appropriate?

2. Are the Panel's accreditation criteria sufficiently flexible to allow agencies to meet their performance requirements, and how does it deal with the requirement for programmes to be evidence-based?

3. How useful is the Panel's advice in the development and delivery of programmes for offenders?

4. What contribution does the Panel make to a culture of effectiveness?

5. What are the costs of the accreditation process, both to agencies and overall?

It is important to emphasise that it was not part of the remit to review the 'What Works' evidence informing JAP's approach to accreditation. There is a large body of literature on the effectiveness of offender treatment programmes, on which a number of critical reflections have already been published.[5] The focus of the evaluation reported here was rather on the processes by which the Panel performed its functions, and its relationship with the prison and probation services and others developing and delivering accredited programmes.

---

5   For a recent edited collection on effective programmes and interventions, see McGuire (2002). For some critical reflections, see Bottoms *et al.,* (2001). Falshaw *et al.* (2003) recently reported on the evaluation of accredited prison-based cognitive skills programmes run between 1996 and 1998. It is understood that the Probation Studies Unit, University of Oxford has recently submitted a report to the Home Office on an evaluation of the Think First accredited general offending behaviour programme, and that this will be published shortly. This will be the first formal evaluation of a JAP accredited programme.

The process-based evaluation was also, necessarily, a 'snapshot' of the Panel's work at a particular period in time. However, the findings have been placed in context by taking into account how the Panel has evolved since its inception, and the likely future developments in its role.

Overall research design

The evaluation took place between December 2001 and September 2002, with data collected from a range of sources up until the end of July 2002. The work comprised three main strands:

- **Documentary.** A review was undertaken of published literature relating to other accreditation models, both in the UK public sector and in the accreditation of offender programmes in other jurisdictions. Documents produced for and by JAP, and other relevant policy documents, were analysed.

- **Contextual Surveys and Interviews.** An analysis of stakeholders' views in prisons and probation areas was carried out, as well as the views of sentencers, programme and treatment providers, and researchers and evaluators. Data for these analyses were obtained through a range of surveys and in-depth interviews (some following up questionnaire responses).

- **Panel observation, interviews and comments.** The Panel was observed in action, and confidential interviews with all members of the Panel were conducted. The JAP meeting during the week beginning 25 of February 2002 was attended, as was the Drugs Sub Panel during the week beginning 27 of May 2002. Panel members received a copy of an Interim Report (submitted in May 2002) and were invited to comment on it individually as research participants. The Drugs Sub Panel meeting offered the opportunity to discuss the Interim Report formally with the Chairman and three members of the Panel. (Additionally comments on the Interim Report from the National Probation Directorate were received). The work of the Panel meeting in September 2002 was not attended or evaluated, as this was outside the period of the data collection.

Further details of these various data sources are given in the next two subsections.

Stakeholders' views

As indicated above, the evaluation is based on analysis of a wide range of stakeholders' views, in addition to observation of the Panel and review of the relevant policy documents and literature. Those serving on the Panel and participating in its decisions have provided an important perspective on its activities. The views were sought of those with a strategic interest in the Panel's work and personnel directly affected by its decisions: policy administrators, programme development managers, and developers of individual programmes seeking accreditation (clearly, there is potentially considerable overlap between these groups). A further perspective comes from local staff in prisons and probation areas supporting or delivering programmes accredited by the Panel: senior managers, programme managers and tutors delivering programmes to offenders, as well as prison personal officers and probation PSR authors and case managers. The survey of programme staff sought quite detailed views about programmes for offenders, and about the work of JAP; the questionnaire to other probation and prison staff was considerably shorter and asked them about their awareness of and sources of information about JAP and accredited programmes. Another perspective was sought from researchers and evaluators through an academic seminar. Finally, questionnaires were used to invite comments from judges and magistrates, and senior sentencers and representatives from the Magistrates' Association were interviewed, about their level of awareness of, and sources of information about accredited programmes, and how this information might influence sentencing decisions. In all cases, names of respondents have been withheld when reporting research data.

To simplify the task of obtaining the views of probation and prison staff, the data collection deliberately concentrated on five regions of the country, selected in consultation with the research steering group. These areas were: North West (Manchester); Eastern (Cambridgeshire); East Midlands (Nottinghamshire); West Midlands (West Mercia); and South East (Thames Valley). The aim was to provide a reasonable geographical spread, a fairly representative selection of types of prison, a metropolitan and urban/rural mix, and varied experiences of accreditation and audit processes. Sentencers from the five areas listed above were surveyed amd interviewed, to maximise fieldwork efficiency. The groups whose perspectives were taken into account in this evaluation are listed in more detail below, together with the numbers sampled and response rates secured:

- **Interviews with JAP members and key policy administrators (JAP interviewees).** Twenty five interviews were completed with appointed and nominated members of the Panel (including one past member) and policy administrators closely involved in the work of the Panel. (There was a 100% response rate among this group, in that no one approached declined to be interviewed). The observations of the February/March 2002 JAP meeting and the May 2002 Drugs Sub Panel Meeting were utilised in interpreting interview data, and in providing a context for that material.

- **Interviews with implementation managers and programme developers.** Eighteen interviews were completed with staff from the National Probation Directorate (NPD) and the Prison Service Sentence Management Group (including the Offending Behaviour Programmes Unit, or OBPU), and prison/probation and independent programme developers (including some who have yet to achieve accreditation, or whose programme was turned down). Again , there was a 100 per cent response rate in this part of the study. Some of these respondents have considerable experience in submitting programmes to JAP, and they provided an important perspective to set alongside that of panel members.

- **Academic seminar.** This seminar took place at the Research Development and Statistics Directorate (RDS) of the Home Office in London. The aim of the seminar was to enable university-based programme developers and evaluators to contribute to the evaluation. Of 14 invited, nine researchers and evaluators were able to participate in the seminar. Although others were sent the seminar materials and invited to comment, unfortunately none were able to do so because of other commitments.

- **Programme staff survey and interviews.** Postal questionnaires were sent to all staff managing and delivering programmes in six prison establishments and five probation areas. Of 254 administered, 167 completed questionnaires were received – a response rate of 66 per cent, which fell below 60 per cent in Greater Manchester (55%) and Thames Valley (53%). This response rate was achieved by sending questionnaires again to non-respondents in areas where initial response rates were particularly low, emphasising the importance of their views and asking them again to complete the questionnaire. Nevertheless, the one-third overall non-response rate has to be borne in mind in interpreting questionnaire results from programme staff. In the analysis of programme staff questionnaires, summarised at Appendix II, respondents are grouped into three staff groups: tutors; line managers; and strategic managers. Questionnaire respondents were also asked to complete a form indicating consent to be interviewed. Forty six members of staff, including senior managers were then interviewed, at subsequent site visits (or in telephone interviews where necessary). Overall, a reasonable cross section of staff groups were interviewed, but unfortunately this was not possible in each individual area or establishment. In all but three sites, at least four members of staff were interviewed, but disappointingly few interviews were secured in Full Sutton prison and the Thames Valley probation area.

- **Ethnic minority programme staff.** Particular efforts were made to identify and obtain the views of ethnic minority programme staff, whilst respecting confidentiality and seeking to avoid making individuals feel singled out.[6] In all, just four completed questionnaires were received from, and three interviews were conducted with, respondents describing themselves as from ethnic groups other than 'white'. Three of these respondents were from Greater Manchester, and one from Nottinghamshire. This no doubt reflects the predominantly white profile of staff overall in the relevant prisons and probation areas (ethnicity profiles were requested from local managers). In Albany, Full Sutton, Drake Hall, and Whatton Prisons, 99 per cent or more staff were described as white. In Manchester Prison and Cambridgeshire Probation Area, the proportion was 97 per cent white; it was 94 per cent in Wellingborough Prison, and 93 per cent in West Mercia Probation Area. The highest ethnic minority representation was reported in Nottinghamshire (87% White) and Greater Manchester (91%) probation areas. So far as we could ascertain, of 37 black and 19 Asian members of staff in Nottinghamshire probation area, only one was working on offender programmes

- **Survey of other prison and probation staff.** A short questionnaire was sent to PSR authors and case managers working in the five probation areas where the views of programme staff were sampled, and to personal (or sentence planning) officers working in five of the six prisons.[7] In achieving the agreed number of administrations, the questionnaire was sent either to all staff within the relevant category in smaller prisons or probation areas, or to a random selection of staff in larger prisons or probation areas. Fifty completed questionnaires were received from 247 sent to prison personal officers, a response rate of around 20 per cent. Unfortunately, of questionnaires sent to around 500 probation staff, mostly by e-mail, only seven completed returns were received, too few to justify any analysis. Unfortunately, the resources to chase up responses to these wider surveys of prison and probation staff were lacking, as securing the highest possible response to the more detailed questionnaire sent to programme staff was seen as the priority. Given the low response rate to the prison staff survey, data from this survey necessarily has to be treated with extreme caution.

6   The approach to seeking views from ethnic minority staff was formulated in consultation with the Panel's diversity advisor.
7   In Wellingborough, all but one of the sentence planning officers were also working on offender programmes.

● **Survey/interviews with sentencers.** With the agreement of the Magistrates' Association, the Lord Chancellor's Department, the Court Service and the Senior Presiding Judge for England and Wales, questionnaires were sent to magistrates and judges in Manchester, Bicester and Reading (both Thames Valley), Worcester and Telford (both West Mercia), Peterborough and Nottingham. Again, questionnaires were sent to all judges, and either to all the magistrates on a bench or to a random selection of the larger benches. Unfortunately, the magistrates' courts in Cambridgeshire (both Peterborough and Cambridge) declined to participate in the survey because of workloads. In total, 177 questionnaires were completed out of 383 (a response rate of 46%), and the target of 40-50 completed questionnaires was achieved in each area where magistrates were surveyed except Nottingham. A total of eight interviews were secured with senior sentencers (of those sought with the Chair of the Bench and Resident judge in each court, and with the Chairs of Council and of the Sentencing Committee of the Magistrates' Association). Unfortunately, interviews could not be arranged in Thames Valley; and there was no Resident judge in Nottingham at the time the fieldwork was being conducted.

As has been seen, very different proportions of the relevant samples described above responded to our research approach (from 100% among JAP members to 1.4% among probation case managers and PSR authors). It cannot be determined whether the views of non-respondents would have differed from those who did respond, but it is reasonable to assume that the lower the response rate, the less representative respondents' views are likely to be. Caution is therefore required in interpreting some of the findings reported below, particularly those relating to prison personal officers.

Other Sources of Data

- **Literature review.** The literature was reviewed relating to the accreditation of offender programmes overseas, and in other public sectors, such as health and education in the UK. An interview with Professor Ellie Scrivens, an expert on accreditation in health care settings and a member of the Scottish Prison Service's Accreditation Panel, was most helpful (see Scrivens, 1995). However, the fact that the Scottish and Canadian systems for accrediting offender programmes have incorporated some aspects of the English model (which effectively began in 1996 with the prison panels – see Chapter 1) necessarily limits what can be learnt through comparison.[8] In other countries, offender programme accreditation is in its early stages: too early for useful comparative analysis.[9] The differing contexts (for example, education or health) in which other public services are accredited also makes direct comparisons with offender programme accreditation quite difficult.[10] Nonetheless, there are some useful parallels, and these will be referred to during the course of the report.

- **Analysis of policy papers.** The JAP documentation which was made available has been used to summarise how programmes have made progress towards Accreditation (see Appendix III). Access was also given to a wide range of other papers, which have been incorporated in the findings and recommendations presented here, for which particular thanks are due to the JAP secretariat, the audit team in HMI Probation, and staff in Prison Service Headquarters and the National Probation Directorate.

---

8   Comparison is also restricted by the different scale of the accreditation activity (covering around 6,000 prisoners in Scotland and 21,000 prisoners and parolees in the Canadian Federal system) and the focus in Canada and Scotland on site accreditation as well as programme accreditation.

9   The Swedish Government is developing accreditation for offender programmes, based on the UK model. Otherwise, the only systematic accreditation it was possible to identify is run by the University of Colorado's Centre for the Prevention and Study of Violence, for 'Blueprints for Violence Prevention' based on methodologically rigorous research.

10 To date, accreditation has been most prevalent in health care and education settings in the US, and it is often individuals or facilities that are accredited rather than programmes. Pickering (1996) summarises the criticisms directed at accreditation in health care: not a panacea; very rarely detects wilful fraud, and preparation takes time. A 1999 Task Force on Accreditation sums up the flaws in US education accreditation systems: goals (protecting public, assuring quality, consultation and protecting professionals) sometimes clash; costs may surpass the value of accreditation; and an inspection mentality can dominate (Gelman *et al.*, 1999).

- **Enrolment of offenders in accredited programmes and completion rates.** One useful indicator for the evaluation is the number of offenders going through accredited programmes in the prison and probation services. In this regard, OBPU has kindly supplemented the data presented in the Prison Service Annual Reports. A copy was also received of the Accredited Programmes Performance Report for 2001/2 circulated by the Head of Interventions NPD to his colleagues in the National Probation Service.

3.   Role and organisation of the Panel

This chapter begins to present the research results. It starts by considering issues relating to the composition of the Panel, a matter that was of considerable topicality during the fieldwork given the imminent recruitment process for the new Panel (now CSAP: see Chapter 1). The second part of the chapter goes on to discuss how meetings were organised and how they functioned (including issues relating to the support given to the Panel).

Panel composition

One important feature of JAP is its independence as 'an advisory body to the correctional services' (according to the paper proposing the new terms of reference). This is reflected both in the fact that the majority of its members are appointed following an open competition, and by the independent appointment of its chairman. As constituted at the time of the research, the Panel comprised 12 appointed members and seven nominated members, listed in Appendix I. The nominated members served on the Panel by virtue of their role in the Home Office, Prison Service or Probation Service. However, others also played a role in Panel meetings, as outlined below.

The ex-officio Panel members from the Probation Service and its Inspectorate (HMIP) were: Professor Rod Morgan (replacing Sir Graham Smith as HM Chief Inspector of Probation); David Perry (Head of Interventions in NPD, formerly the Probation Unit of the Home Office); and Andrew Underdown (originally representing the former Association of Chief Officers of Probation, ACOP). As NPD commented in responding to the Interim Report, these were the three bodies that originally promoted the 'What Works' agenda in the probation service, leading to the development of the joint Prison/Probation Panel. The three bodies represented three different strands of working with offenders in the community: independent inspection and audit (HMIP); areas and organisational delivery (ACOP); and policy and development links with government (Probation Unit/NPD).

Panel membership from the Prison Service originally consisted of Danny Clark (former head of Prison Research) and David Thornton (former head of OBPU). When Danny Clark moved to become a programme development manager in the NPD, it was considered that his research knowledge enabled him to remain as an 'independent' Panel member. The Prison Service nominated membership at the time of the evaluation was: Elizabeth Barnard (head of What Works Unit) and Peter Atkinson (Prison Governor, invited to attend the Panel to mirror Andrew Underdown).

However, other developments had blurred the distinction between Panel membership and participation in meetings. Since taking up his strategic role as Head of Interventions in NPD, David Perry's attendance at the Panel has mirrored that of his counterpart in the Prison Service, Nigel Newcomen, head of the Sentence Management Group (not a Panel member), in providing context-setting material at the first and last sessions of each Panel week but taking no active part in considering programme submissions. (To confuse matters, however, David Perry remained technically a member of the Panel.) Meg Blumson, as head of Offending Behaviour programmes in NPD, therefore joined the Panel in place of David Perry, but without full membership. Trish Wincote replaced David Thornton as head of OBPU and was brought onto the Panel, but similarly without being appointed as a full Panel member. There were thus, in practice, four active participants in Panel meetings from probation (Rod Morgan, Andrew Underdown, and Danny Clark as full members, plus Meg Blumson) and three from the Prison Service (Elizabeth Barnard and Peter Atkinson as full members, plus Trish Wincote).

Chris Lewis (Home Office, RDS) was the final nominated member, and the research resource to which he gave the Panel access was clearly valued by his colleagues. Additionally, however, the Panel had engaged the ongoing services of two advisors for particular programmes or policies on which it felt it needed additional expertise: they were Diane Baderin (head of Diversity, NPD), who had a permanent role as the diversity advisor for the Panel; and Professor Michael Gossop of the National Addiction Centre, who acted as an advisor on drugs programmes (given the prominence of such programmes in the Panel's business). Other outside advisors were occasionally engaged on a more ad hoc basis, for example when the Panel was considering applications for accreditation in relation to 'enhanced community punishment', or from a therapeutic community.

The effect of the incremental growth outlined above is that, at the time of the research, four additional people regularly attended panel meetings (Trish Wincote, Meg Blumson, Diane Baderin and Michael Gossop) whom it was difficult to distinguish from Panel members. This changed the apparent balance between participants who were Panel members appointed following a competitive process (13, including Sir Duncan Nichol) and those brought in by some other route (10 plus David Perry and Nigel Newcomen). There was comment during interviews that the composition of the Panel might have become somewhat weighted towards officials within the relevant agencies, with implications for the body's apparent independence.

Turning now to the appointed members, these included five specialists in sex offender programmes (Hilary Eldridge, Dawn Fisher, Don Grubin, Janice Marques and Bill Murphy). Three appointed members had a special expertise in the drugs field (Norman Hoffman, Doug Lipton and Simon Shepherd), and the remaining four were generalists (Moira Hamlin, Mike Maguire, Frank Porporino and Peter Raynor). Five of the appointed members were from outside the UK.

As previously noted, the recruitment of new appointed and nominated members of the Panel was being undertaken at the time of the research. The intention was to reduce the permanent nominated membership to three, with other nominated members attending as required by the agenda. The aim appeared to be to restore the independent balance of the Panel, and to provide the relevant policy input as and when required. However, one question raised during the interviews was whether only full membership of the Panel should confer 'voting' rights. The independent nature of the Panel, it was thought by some respondents, would be most clearly delineated if its decisions were the preserve of its full members (whether appointed or nominated), with others attending in a purely advisory capacity.

As regards the new appointed members, experts were being sought in a wider range of fields (with fewer specialists in sex offender programmes). These plans addressed some of the points raised in interviews, where Panel members thought that the Panel's future involvement in sex offender programmes would be diminished, and that this change called for a reassessment of the balance between areas of expertise. Another view was that the Panel required more expertise in drug and alcohol programmes – in the clinical area rather than in assessment or research – among its membership. Respondents also identified a need for more expertise related to programme delivery and 'operational' matters (for example, what it was like to actually run a programme in a prison). The ability of the Panel to give proper attention to the requirements for staff training was raised at the academic seminar (if not through Panel membership, then through devolving this responsibility to another body). The importance of maintaining a focus on quality was emphasised, and here academics were seen to have played a major role in ensuring adherence to 'What Works' principles. This, it was said, argued for preserving a major academic component in JAP membership (albeit one that reflected the broader ambit of the Panel's work as it moved into the 'integrated systems' agenda: see Chapter 1).

One source of potential tension identified in interviews was the presence on the Panel of some programme developers, whose ability to judge programme content was seen as crucial. Nonetheless, an apparent conflict arose when the Panel was considering a programme that a Panel member had played some part in developing. In the eyes of programme developers and programme staff, this issue was very contentious. Such respondents may not always have been aware of the internal mechanisms utilised within the Panel to attempt to prevent potential conflicts of interest by excluding any Panel member with an interest from attending the particular sub-panel considering that application. (Interests had to be declared under the Code of Practice for Panel members.) Even where respondents were aware of these mechanisms, it was often thought that there might be pressure to view favourably a submission to which a Panel member was known to have contributed. One suggestion was that, having acted as a consultant on a programme, a JAP member might need to withdraw from his or her membership of the Panel for a period.

Of the other views expressed by JAP members, perhaps the strongest was the need for a more ethnically diverse membership, an important point given the emphasis given to race equality in the Race Relations (Amendment) Act 2000. Recruitment for the new Panel sought to address this issue, by encouraging candidates from ethnic minority backgrounds. However, NPD's response to the Interim Report noted potential tensions between ensuring balance in the ethnicity of Panel membership and ensuring that the Panel comprised leading experts in their fields. The suggestion was that another way of ensuring that Panel members had the capability to consider diversity might be to require applicants to demonstrate their commitment to the diversity agenda, and to show how they had helped to promote this agenda in their work.

The general literature on accreditation programmes offers relatively generic advice on Panel composition. Generally, the importance of including well-qualified, highly respected individuals is underscored. Individuals who are currently practising in the field are also valued, given their understanding of changes in the relevant legal, clinical and political environments. The overall size of the group must be workable, sufficient to cover the tasks and provide the necessary range of expertise and representation of viewpoints.

In looking to the composition of the accreditation panels in Canada and Scotland, one can draw some comparisons with JAP:

- In order to cover the range of subject matters, *Canada* uses an International Expert Panel with seven members to set general policy, then relies on Individual Subject Panels to review individual programme areas. The subject panels include three members from the Expert Panel (to maintain consistency of mission and focus) with three specialists in the particular area.

- The *Canadian* system extends more general conflict of interest provisions by prohibiting Subject Panel members from having a previous or current connection with the management or development of a Correctional Service of Canada programme.

- The chairs of the Canadian and Scottish Panels are not independent. In *Scotland*, the Panel is chaired by a member of the Prison Service Board; in *Canada*, an assistant Commissioner of the Canadian Correctional Service chairs the Panel.

- The *Scottish* Prison Service panel is relatively small in comparison with the others (eight members in total), and includes five individuals from outside the service: two with professional qualifications in psychology and offending behaviour programmes; two social workers with experience in offending behaviour; and one person with experience in public sector accreditation. By having two people with overlapping areas of experience, the Panel can function when some members cannot attend. The current mix of expertise is not seen as fixed for the future, and it is envisaged that the Panel composition might change as the need arises.

Meeting arrangements and functioning

The general view from panel members was that two week-long meetings of the entire Panel each year enabled them to balance other commitments with the need to get through JAP business (the lengthier meetings in the early days of the Panel were universally regarded as overly-long and exhausting). However, there was an acceptance that the main Panel meetings needed to be supplemented by additional meetings of the formally constituted standing sub panels (the drugs sub panel was cited as having a particularly heavy workload). UK-based Panel members also frequently committed themselves to a range of other activities outside main Panel meetings: for example, visits to programme developers to advise on feedback on submissions, as well as visits to prison and probation areas. In these circumstances, it is difficult to see how it would be possible for the main Panel to meet more frequently than twice yearly. The cost implications of additional meetings would also need to be borne in mind, as discussed in Chapter 4 below.

A slightly different issue is the interaction between the main Panel and its sub panels (both the more formally constituted Drugs and Audit sub panels and the less formal 'sub panels' or working groups assigned to work on particular submissions during a meeting of the full Panel). One question is whether JAP should conduct more of its business through formal sub panel meetings. Here, Panel members expressed little enthusiasm for a model similar to the Canadian smaller Expert Panel with separate specialist Subject Panels. They valued the coherence and equal status conferred by common membership of the main Panel.

JAP members did, however, express some concerns were about the functioning of the main Panel and sub panels, and suggestions were made for improvement. Some Panel members seemed more comfortable participating in smaller group discussion than in the larger – and more unwieldy – forum of the main Panel. The meeting of the full Panel on the final morning of each week was seen as an occasion for important decisions when the Panel was asked to endorse sub panel recommendations; yet time constraints and fatigue made it difficult to do full justice to the business. It was suggested that energy levels and focus might be better maintained by interspersing plenary and sub panel meetings during the week, to enable a sub panel to give an issue more detailed consideration and bring proposals to a main Panel meeting.

Programme developers (and programme development/implementation managers) described mixed experiences of attending sub panels (although the accounts received related to different periods during the Panel's history). Some found the experience intimidating and confusing, although there were also accounts of individual Panel members being very helpful and constructive during discussion. Interviewees found it helpful to know the identity of the participants in the sub panel (the guidance for sub panel chairs issued for the February/March 2002 JAP meeting requests introductions to be made), and they expressed a wish for greater clarity as to what the sub panel was looking for from them. Some found the discussion disappointing – a tendency for academic 'debating' points to dominate; too little structure to the discussion; and a lack of familiarity with submission material were amongst the criticisms. This last point is of some significance in the context of the literature on procedural justice, discussed in Chapter 6. Programme developers typically spent many hours developing the five programme manuals that the Panel required for a formal submission (see Chapter 1); understandably, if panel members were then unfamiliar with some of the materials, there was a tendency among programme developers to see themselves as having been judged without their case having been fully and carefully considered.

A separate point was the potential lack of continuity in ad hoc sub panel decisions over time, particularly where there was a change of membership. Some Panel members expressed concern that a fresh sub panel, considering an application for accreditation, might disagree with the views previously offered by a differently constituted sub panel that had considered an application for advice; or the fresh sub panel might raise new points (although no instances of where this had happened were given). Greater continuity in sub panel membership was therefore seen as desirable. In some of the sub panels that were observed, documentation was not easily available on previous decisions related to a programme, and time was spent trying to reconstruct the history. For example, difficulties were observed in one sub panel in reviewing the history of an 'enhanced community punishment scheme'; an earlier submission had been entitled 'applying accreditation criteria to community service', and this name change created temporary confusion. Needless to say, these kinds of issues were apparent to programme developers, who referred to sub panels as "moving the goal posts", changing their minds, raising new points or forgetting previous decisions. There was some feeling amongst programme developers that the deliberations at sub panel meetings should be minuted to provide a more detailed record than the formal feedback letter they received. The sessions during which a sub panel met to comment on the draft feedback letter were sometimes observed to be hampered by debates over fairly minor drafting points rather than issues of substance (to which there sometimes appeared to be too little time to devote adequate attention). It might be more effective – and place less pressure on the letter-writer – if a draft approved by the sub panel chair was circulated for written comments instead.[11]

A related concern raised by Panel members was that their areas of expertise did not always fit the sub panels to which they were allocated, and some were mystified how allocation decisions were made. The new (2002) guidance for sub panel chairs was seen as likely to improve consistency between different sub panels on matters of process, but did not address more substantive issues of consistency in decisions. One suggestion was to arrange a meeting of sub panel chairs at some point during the week to talk over common issues.

Support and advice to the Panel

The above discussion touches on the support provided by the JAP secretariat, and other sources of support and advice for the Panel. Overall, levels of satisfaction were high here, with Panel members – and others – pointing to marked improvements in secretariat support since the introduction of a dedicated post and increased resources. Where there had been difficulties with the practicalities of JAP meetings, these were seen as the natural product of human error given the size of the administrative task involved. In view of the earlier comments about consistency between sub panel meetings, a system for tracking submissions through the Panel, many thought, would be extremely helpful, perhaps using a simple data base to record the kind of details summarised at Appendix III. This could be developed in such a way as to provide each sub panel with a digest of previous decisions, perhaps with

---

11 Letter writers were usually drawn from RDS staff, who might be completely new to the work of the Panel or not encounter it in the normal course of their duties.

entries on which panel members participated in those decisions. Again, this would assist letter writers, who might not have worked with that particular sub panel before.

When it came to sources of advice, appreciation was expressed about the quality of advice brought in, for example, by seconded experts on drugs programmes, therapeutic communities and community punishment. The appointment of a dedicated diversity advisor provoked a range of comments. The sustained attention to this topic that the advisor's presence brought was valued, and it was thought by some that this should be reflected in the Panel's own advice to programme developers (discussed under accreditation criteria in Chapter 4). However, views diverged on whether a diversity advisor should feel able to contribute to more general discussions, and there was a hint from some that the appointment of a specialist advisor detracted from JAP members' own responsibility for examining questions relating to diversity.

Two areas were specifically mentioned where, in the opinion of Panel members, further advice would be valuable. These were, first, research briefings to enable Panel members to remain up to date with the relevant technical literature on the range of programmes coming before JAP; and secondly, ethics advice. This latter suggestion arose in respect of the possible impact of psychodrama on offenders, which was seen to raise a wider need to ensure that offenders were not damaged through participation in confrontational and demanding processes.

Conclusions and recommendations

On the future composition of the Panel, many of the points raised by stakeholders were being addressed in the recruitment exercise for the new Panel (e.g. the need to preserve independence and quality, and for a more diverse membership in terms of expertise and ethnicity). Having restored the independent make-up of the Panel by reducing the ex-officio membership to three (from 11 current participants, some of whose status is unclear), it will be important to ensure that this independence is underlined in the future. One way in which to achieve this is to make a clear distinction between full Panel members and co-opted participants, who otherwise may over time and with frequent attendance acquire the apparent de facto status of Panel membership.

First recommendation: Introduce a clear distinction between full Panel members, whether appointed or nominated, and other participants. Consider: only full members to have 'voting' rights; only full members to act as sub panel chairs; previewers or shepherds (see Chapter 4) to be selected from full membership.

Another way in which the Panel can underscore its independence is by clarifying the arrangements to avoid conflicts of interest, and ensuring that these arrangements are appropriately publicised. This was a significant concern amongst programme developers and programme staff, some of whom thought there might be pressure to view favourably a submission to which a Panel member had contributed, even though the member in question was excluded from the relevant sub panel. Such pressure might be lessened if the Panel member did not attend the relevant JAP week, or withdrew his or her membership for a short period. We suggest that the Panel would visibly strike a better balance between the need for probity and the value of having programme developers on its membership if it adopted a more stringent rule requiring temporary withdrawal from panel attendance or membership.

Second recommendation: Clarify/publicise the arrangements to prevent potential conflicts of interest when the Panel is considering a submission in which a member has an interest, or what might be construed as an interest. Consider requiring a Panel member who has acted as consultant to a programme to withdraw from Panel membership for a period, to ensure that he or she does not attend the Panel week in which the programme is being considered.

Generally, the Panel was seen as functioning well, particularly in sub panel sessions. Recent improvements were identified; indeed, some were brought in during the course of the evaluation: increased secretariat resources; better guidance for letter writers and for sub panel chairs. However, both JAP members and programme developers perceived a need for greater continuity in sub panels whose membership might change over time. Suggestions for improving functioning and continuity included interspersing plenary and sub panel meetings during the JAP week and arranging a meeting of sub panel chairs at some point during the week. A need was also identified for additional advice through research briefings to up date Panel members on recent literature relating to the range of programmes coming before them, and on ethical questions raised by certain aspects of programmes. In the light of the concerns raised by interviews and our own observations, we recommend as follows:

Third recommendation: Improve JAP paperwork management and introduce clearer records of sub panel discussion and decisions. Consider setting up a database to track submissions through the Panel, and provide sub panels with a digest of previous decisions and who contributed to them.

4.   Accrediting programmes

The process of accreditation formed the predominant activity of the Panel, which accredited 15 programmes in just over two years, and in six full JAP meetings (between its first meeting in November/December 1999 and the one observed in February/March 2002). In addition, the Panel granted two programmes 'recognised' status, and advised that work on two programmes should be discontinued. The earlier Prison Service General Accreditation Panel had accredited the Therapeutic Community at HM Grendon, and JAP approved the 'audit of delivery' document for this programme. This compares with 15 accredited programmes and 22 accredited sites in Scotland, and six accredited programmes (42 sites) in Canada.[12]

This chapter looks at various issues relating to the performance of the Panel in its main function of accrediting programmes. It starts with a consideration of the programmes that achieved accreditation.

Progress of programmes towards accreditation

The progress of programmes that attained accredited status is presented at Appendix III, which summarises the Panel's actions. In brief:

- Seven programmes achieved accreditation at their first formal submission for that status (four following earlier 'advice' from the Panel).

- Seven programmes achieved accreditation at their second formal submission (four of which were separately submitted for advice at least once).

- One programme required three formal submissions before gaining accredited status (following initial advice from the Panel).

---

12 The JAP does not accredit sites; instead the delivery of accredited programmes on site is audited under arrangements approved by the Panel (see Chapter 5).

Looking at types of programmes accredited by the Panel (future references will be by the acronyms used here):

- *Sex Offender (six)*: Three Prison Service programmes – Sex Offender Treatment Programme (SOTP), plus the Rolling and Extended versions of this programme (the Rolling programme after three formal submissions, the others at their first formal submission). The West Midlands, Thames Valley and Northumbria probation programmes (all on their first formal submission following initial advice).

- *General Offending Behaviour (five)*: Enhanced Thinking Skills (ETS) and Reasoning and Rehabilitation (R&R) on their first submission; Cognitive Self Change (CSCP) and Priestly One-to-One on their second, following initial advice; Think First (TF) on its second submission (following advice on the draft resubmission document).

- *Others (four)*: South Yorkshire Drink Impaired Drivers (DIDS) on its second submission following initial advice; Wiltshire Aggression Replacement Training (ART) on its second submission following two submissions for advice; the substance abuse treatment programme developed by the Rehabilitation of Addicted Prisoners Trust (RAPT), and Controlling Anger and Learning to Manage it (CALM) on their second submission. RAPT was the only non-prison or probation service programme to be accredited.

Accreditation process

In their descriptions of how they approached accreditation, Panel members placed considerable stress on what they saw as the constructive, collaborative spirit in which they engaged in the task. Their aim was to read material carefully, to offer good advice and to act fairly. Although they had criticisms, programme developers too saw many aspects of the accreditation process as constructive and positive. Feedback letters were generally seen as progressive and helpful, and accounts were given of individual Panel members giving considerable support to programme developers in interpreting the Panel's comments and requirements.

Panel members generally received programme submissions as they convened for JAP meetings, rather than in advance, and seemed somewhat constrained by having to absorb a large amount of material (five manuals plus appendices) during the busy JAP week. Indeed, some saw this as restricting their capacity adequately to judge how a programme might run in practice, and suggested that it might be helpful to learn about programmes through site visits or non-paper material (e.g. videos or presentations). Several programme developers, in attending Panel meetings, were aware that JAP members had had insufficient time thoroughly to read and digest the volume of paperwork in a submission. As a consequence, they felt, Panel members showed a lack of engagement with, or sometimes misinterpreted, the material, or they might over-emphasise certain specific points because they had not had time to reflect on the submission as a whole. Some applicants saw it as their responsibility to assist the Panel by cutting down on detail and focusing on the few key issues on which they needed comments and advice, perhaps offering a presentation to the relevant sub panel to bring out the salient issues. However, a certain amount of frustration was expressed by those who perceived themselves as having worked hard to meet submission deadlines and produce a great deal of material only to discover that it was not fully read in advance of meetings.

Given these views, one strong suggestion that seemed to emerge from interviews with JAP members was the potential benefit of a detailed preview of material by one or two representatives of the sub panel (perhaps in the context of a site visit) prior to the consideration of a submission at a meeting. Although it would incur additional fees for the previewer(s), it was believed that this would make meetings more efficient and effective. A similar approach was agreed by the full Panel at its meeting on Friday 1 March 2002, to deal with a situation where requirements are attached to the award of accreditation, which have to be met within a specified period in order to retain accredited status. The Panel approved the nomination of a 'shepherd' to confirm that the requirements were met if the secretariat advised that this was outside its technical competence in a particular case.

Another point of common agreement was the importance of maintaining high standards for programmes seeking accreditation. For JAP members, this was tempered by a wish to avoid being over-exacting, in effect creating a hurdle that made accredited status virtually unattainable. In general, Panel members thought the Chairman set the right tone in emphasising both the need for quality and the 'real world' of programme delivery and finite resources. Programme developers were also supportive of the standards set by the Panel in applying the criteria. Some saw the quality assurance provided by accreditation as important in attracting the necessary resources to ensure that programmes were run properly. However, others were concerned that accreditation might prove an impossible hurdle for some programmes. Some programme developers considered that different standards were applied to comparable programmes, and had gained the impression that Panel members occasionally engaged in academic debate in sub panel meetings, or allowed their field of expertise to dominate their reactions to a submission.

Panel members depicted themselves as adopting a flexible, common sense approach to the requirement for a model of change based on evidence or a reasonable hypothesis. More complex issues arose over applications in relation to which there was, to date, a lack of strong evidence in the research literature. Where the prison and probation services needed to move forward on a particular approach, for which there was not yet a solid evidence base, it was generally considered possible to apply learning from similar approaches to give a programme 'recognised' status pending the collection of reconviction data. Against this, reservations were expressed by some academic researchers on the panel as to whether sufficient time was being allowed for the careful collection of evidence necessary before programmes were implemented, and the suggestion that JAP could be doing more to encourage rigour in the evidence required before a programme was rolled-out nationally.

JAP members reported considerable consensus over where the research evidence pointed in relation to general offending behaviour programmes, sex offender programmes and democratic Therapeutic Communities. There was much less consensus in relation to drugs programmes, raising questions over which it was difficult to adjudicate, particularly for JAP members without expertise in the relevant area. From the programme developers' perspective, these issues were seen to create sticking points in getting programmes accredited, as Panel time was given to lengthy debate about the evidence of effectiveness rather than giving 'What Works'-based feedback and guidance to applicants. In addition, a variety of programme developers perceived real practical difficulties in producing adequate research evidence in relation to certain offender groups, citing women, racially motivated offenders and psychopaths.

The stance taken by the Panel in insisting upon high standards seems to have the support of programme staff who completed the questionnaire (see Appendix II). Mostly lacking direct experience of the accreditation process, they described the Panel as performing a 'quality control' role, although a higher proportion of managers than tutors depicted the Panel in this way. Only eight per cent of programme staff saw the Panel as distant or disconnected from practice – nine per cent of tutors, 14 per cent of line managers, and no strategic managers. Although a small and possibly unrepresentative sample, of whom relatively few had previously heard of JAP, prison personal officers also saw the Panel's role in terms of quality control and monitoring.

There was also a positive, although guarded, reaction to JAP's decisions on individual programmes from programme staff. Of the programme staff who answered this question, only five per cent rated the Panel's decisions as poor or very poor, and 49 per cent saw them as good or very good. However, no fewer than 46 per cent were neutral on this point, and 26 per cent of the respondents did not answer the question. Additional comments on accreditation decisions by JAP were mostly positive, pointing to an objective approach and approval of effective and workable programmes. However, some concerns were expressed about the 'white male' focus of some programmes. Questions of diversity are explored in further detail later in this chapter, drawing on the views of Panel members, programme developers and researchers as well as programme staff.

Submitting programmes

Panel members readily expressed views about the qualities of a submission that was likely to succeed. Intellectual coherence between the different manuals and elements of the programme was considered desirable. Clarity was a key requirement according to a number of Panel members, and a succinct, straightforward written style was prized. The starting point was a clear model of change in the theory manual, based on a good grasp of the relevant literature and evidence. The programme manual should follow from the model of change, rather than the other way round, so that the submission demonstrated that people knew what they were doing and why they were doing it. Weak submissions were defined by the absence of these qualities. One problem identified by Panel members was where an academic prepared the theory manual with an inadequate understanding of the actual programme content, producing a dislocation between the practical exercises and the supposed theory behind them. Some models of change were seen as inspired by ideology rather than by an appreciation of the current literature. Another temptation to which programme developers sometimes succumbed, in the view of Panel members, was to include everything they knew about the area in the theory manual, without developing an integrated model of change.

One issue about which there was a substantial amount of discussion was the role of the NPD and OBPU in providing an interface between the Panel and the field to ensure that accreditation was pursued in accordance with agency priorities, and to assure quality in the programmes submitted to the Panel. The 'triangular' relationship between Panel, gatekeeper (or 'sponsor') and programme developer, though necessary, was seen as creating tensions, and it was difficult to strike the right balance between setting agency priorities on the one hand, and over-controlling access to what was an independent Panel on the other. Private and non-profit making organisations did not have to go through the gatekeeping process, so independent access was assured, but in general such bodies were seen as disadvantaged by lacking the infrastructure and resources to commission the expertise and research necessary to put together a convincing application.

It was widely seen as the correctional services' responsibility to determine their requirements for offender treatment and to target Panel resources accordingly, though this was a function they were not always seen as carrying out effectively. Both JAP interviewees and programme developers saw the development of prisons drugs programmes and their submission to the Panel as having been poorly co-ordinated (or not co-ordinated) in the past. Although the Drugs Strategy Unit (DSU) in the Prisons Service was perceived now to be formulating a more strategic approach, it was thought to be hampered by a legacy of confusion over which of the numerous programmes that had been allowed to develop should be put forward for accreditation. On a different point, one programme developer argued that the choice of accredited programmes in the areas of general offending behaviour, violence and impaired driving was restricted when compared with the range of programmes developed for the comparatively small sex offender population.

Gatekeepers were sometimes faulted for being insufficiently proactive in managing the submission of programmes to the Panel, and not consistently communicating with programme providers about the requirements and expectations of the Panel. The inevitable consequence was a certain amount of wastage, although interviewees also suggested that the gatekeeper was an evolving role and that its performance – and credibility with the field – had considerably improved with experience. A few programme developers raised concerns about access to the Panel becoming a bureaucratic rather than an 'objective' decision, and saw prison and probation service gatekeepers as impeding their access to the Panel and obscuring the Panel's requirements. The role of gatekeepers is revisited in Chapter 6 below.

People with experience of submitting programmes to the Panel were asked about their understanding of JAP's requirements, and their reactions towards the comments made by the Panel – whether the rationale was clear, and whether the comments were fair and useful. In interpreting their views, it needs to be borne in mind that interviewees were discussing contact with the Panel at different stages in its history, and were not always aware of how procedures had evolved since their own experiences.

Most programme developers found the criteria helpful in setting out expectations, and some were able to draw on their own experience or that of colleagues, or use earlier submissions as a guide, in putting together submissions. However, others felt a need for more guidance as to what to include in the various manuals, and how to structure their submissions, particularly when they were putting forward novel approaches. Over-prescription, for example on document length, was not desired, but some interviewees thought it would be helpful to be able to follow a pro-forma or to be supplied with examples of what the Panel found helpful or unhelpful in a submission. It was also suggested that some panel time might be set aside for early advice sessions where programme developers could consult individual Panel members about the requirements; this consultation might be provided through site visits to enable Panel members to gain an appreciation of how the programme was run on-the-ground.

Although the formal feedback letter from the Panel was described by some programme developers as constructive and encouraging, written comments were not always seen as sufficiently clear and precise. Programme developers would have appreciated a clearer distinction between recommendations whose implementation was crucial in order to gain accreditation and helpful suggestions on how to improve the programme. Some recipients perceived the letter as being somewhat critical or cautious in tone. It was suggested that it could be split into three sections – one covering compliance with 'What Works' principles; a second providing clinical suggestions on how the programme might be improved; and the third listing typographical or grammatical mistakes in submission documents. More often than not, programme developers saw panel comments as useful and fair. However, some believed the models offered in their programmes had been dismissed prematurely without an understanding of the underlying rationale (although there were also comments that JAP had become more open to different approaches). One interviewee provided an insight into programme developers' immediate reactions to the JAP letter: 'we all felt quite dreadful … like every human reaction, you don't see the good bits to begin with, you just see all the difficulties'. This is a useful reminder of the emotional dimensions that inevitably accompany a process such as accreditation,[13] underlining the need for fairness to be apparent in Panel procedures. This point to is revisited in Chapter 6.

Accreditation criteria

At the time of the research, JAP used eleven criteria to make decisions about programme accreditation and advise on programmes being developed for accreditation (listed in Appendix I). A programme could score a maximum of two on each criterion, and in order to be accredited, a maximum score was mandatory on six criteria, namely: model of change; selection of offenders; targeting dynamic risk factors; continuity of programmes and services; ongoing monitoring; and ongoing evaluation. A programme required a minimum total score of 19 (out of 22) to achieve accredited status; a score of 17 normally conferred 'recognised' status, and 12 normally marked a programme as 'promising'. Two of the criteria – targeting dynamic risk factors and range of factors – were combined in the

13 See Barbalet (1998) on the way in which certain social structures are intrinsically connected to emotions.

revised criteria approved by the main Panel on 1 March 2002, a change requiring adjustment of total scores associated with accreditation decisions. A comparison of the criteria used by JAP with those used in Scotland and Canada shows striking similarities both in scope and in specifics, except that 'effective methods' is mandatory in Canada, and Scotland appears to have a more strictly cognitive behavioural focus. The relative congruence across different jurisdictions is hardly surprising given the tendency for the Panels to import one another's practice.

JAP interviewees depicted the criteria as a flexible and workable tool (though one that had initially been off-putting for some). Concerns and differences of view were expressed, some of which are resolved by the new criteria, generally seen as an improvement – especially in making the criteria less repetitive and more accessible to applicants. For example, several Panel members thought the new criteria would be more easily applicable to approaches outside cognitive behavioural techniques, such as therapeutic communities. Diversity was seen as more fully accommodated in the new criteria, but some proposals were made for further development (discussed below). One suggestion at the academic seminar was for a greater emphasis on community integration, and how to assist offenders to take up the opportunities that might be available.

Showing limited awareness that the criteria were to be revised, some programme developers were frustrated by what they perceived as a cognitive-behavioural bias in the criteria (or in how they were applied by the Panel); others described re-packaging their submissions to fit a cognitive behavioural model. Some believed the criteria set expectations that certain programme designs would never be able to meet, for example because their emphasis was not on skills training or because they could not guarantee follow-up in the community for short term prisoners released without licence.

Panel members generally regarded the scoring system for accreditation as appropriate, the point being made that it ruled out the approval of a programme with a major flaw, which would fail a number of individual criteria. One doubt raised was that the maximum score of two for each criterion provided little scope for fine judgement, nor did it differentiate the relative importance of various criteria (beyond the items on which a score of two was mandatory). On the other hand, there was resistance to wholesale change of the scoring mechanism on the grounds that this might introduce undue complexity. A specific suggestion was to introduce an 'approved' status below 'recognised', where a model had been piloted but needed more than 12 months for the systematic collection of data before full accreditation was considered.

Programme staff reported a fair amount of knowledge about the accreditation criteria (63% had a least 'some' knowledge, though 49% of tutors said they had 'no knowledge'). They expressed positive views – perhaps more so than Panel members might have expected. Seventy-nine per cent agreed that the criteria 'set high standards that increase the likelihood of effectiveness', and only 14 per cent that they 'set unreasonable expectations'. Very few (6%) saw the criteria as 'too vague in specifying what is required'. On the other hand, almost two-fifths (39%) of the staff answering this question thought that the criteria were 'about right in improving the quality of programmes'.

Diversity was an issue, with only a quarter of programme staff responding to the survey agreeing that the standards set by the criteria were applicable to all offenders, and two-fifths believing that they failed to take account of the needs of some offenders. Additional comments related more often to diversity than any other issue, with respondents expressing the view that some programmes did not meet the needs, variously, of ethnic minorities, women, or individuals with learning difficulties, disabilities or hearing impairment. The matter of diversity is considered next.

Diversity

Both JAP interviewees and programme developers saw the needs of women and ethnic minorities as presenting a challenge with which there had been some reluctance to engage. Programme developers were described by JAP interviewees as claiming that programme materials were culturally neutral or referring to a lack of evidence about their impact on certain groups. Conversely, JAP members were depicted by programme developers as conceding that there was a lack of evidence, for example about the applicability of cognitive behavioural methods to women, yet being reluctant to consider other models. As acknowledged at the academic seminar, there remains a real lack of evidence relating to diversity.[14] Unfortunately, in its absence, belief and assertion has tended to acquire the status of 'truth', as was discovered in the data collection.

Some interviewees involved in the accreditation process perceived a lack of open debate on the topic of diversity. In their view, there was not a 'receptive environment' for this (despite a Prisons/Probation Diversity Review of programme material conducted during 2002, on which

---

14 Reporting the paucity of female samples in the primary studies on which 'What Works' knowledge is based, and the failure consistently to code ethnicity either in the studies or in meta-analyses, McGuire (2002: 30) concludes that:
    There is a requirement for more careful study of the kind of variations that might need to be made in programmes to accommodate diversity amongst participants. This needs to take account of variations in age, gender, ethnicity or other cultural differences. It also needs to focus on the adaptation of materials for people with literacy problems, communication problems or learning disabilities.

a report was submitted to the Panel at its September 2002 meeting). A few programme developers thought that the recent emphasis on diversity questions suggested that the issue had, rightly, gained more prominence, but it also created the impression of moving goal posts. At the academic seminar, it was argued that a focus on problem solving in programmes might not meet the criminogenic needs of Asian or black offenders, or reflect their experiences of exclusion. However, some seminar participants firmly rebutted the argument that 'What Works' research had been done exclusively on white male offenders; many of the studies had included large proportions of males of black or Hispanic origins – both well-represented amongst criminal justice populations in North America (but see footnote 14). Yet it was also recognised that in relation to some types of programmes – such as resettlement – the effect of cultural context for different ethnic groups needed to be taken into account.

In the absence of an 'agreed' treatment model for women, a significant concern was that women were being denied access to whatever programmes were available as a result of a failure to resolve debates such as the appropriateness or otherwise of single sex groups. Offenders lacking in basic skills were another group that was described as neglected by programme developers to date, being excluded from mainstream programmes because of the need for conceptual skills as well as reading and writing. It was argued that lessons could be drawn from educational psychology or other literature from the education field on how to cater for individuals with special needs, and indeed for offenders with negative school experiences.

The NPD and RDS have commissioned research to look at the literacy requirements for the current suite of community-based general offending programmes. Research is also in progress on the criminogenic needs, and the experiences of supervision, of black and Asian offenders, in addition to the evaluation of pathfinder projects for these groups (some of these developments are reviewed in Powis and Walmsley (2002). Unfortunately, there seemed little awareness of these initiatives among most of the people interviewed.

There was a debate among respondents about how to accommodate diversity in the accreditation criteria. One argument was for a 'diversity criterion', focusing specifically on whether programme content was suitable for different groups. Another was that the answer lay not in further adjustment of the criteria, but in careful monitoring of how diversity was addressed in the choice of methods and exercises, or in the implementation and delivery of programmes. Other views were that the criterion relating to programme content should cover adjustments to accommodate cultural diversity, and that further advice was required under selection, engagement and motivation of offenders on how to meet different ethnic and cultural needs.

Of 46 interviewed, only four members of programme staff – all from the Prison Service – believed that programme material was relevant to all offenders irrespective of gender or ethnicity. Half the interviewees (24) raised ethnicity as an issue, and it was given equal prominence within both prison and probation services. A problem cited by some interviewees was the use of inappropriate scenarios in programme materials, based on white culture, for example a situation occurring in a pub or an exercise involving the acronym P.I.G. (since changed following the Diversity Review mentioned above). Views differed as to whether it was possible to adapt programme material to incorporate more culturally relevant or sensitive examples or whether programmes effectively needed to be redesigned. A few practitioners said they had relayed their concerns about the use of inappropriate names or scenarios in ETS and TF to headquarters staff, but perceived a lack of progress towards change (again, apparently unaware of the Diversity Review then underway).

Gender was mentioned by 16 interviewed probation programme staff (most prison staff were working in male only establishments). Again, there was a difference of view as to whether programmes could be adapted to accommodate women, or were simply inappropriate to their thinking patterns and criminogenic needs. One manager characterised the approach as 'trying to squeeze women into a male model of change with a token gesture of not having any women on their own in [male dominated] groups'. One practitioner was mystified by the decision to apply TF to women, since he gathered it was a programme designed for men. A female practitioner thought that ETS processes were equally applicable to women as to men, although scenarios needed adjustment, and noted that women often performed better because they were more open to reviewing their thinking.

Fifteen programme staff referred to the absence of provision for offenders lacking in basic skills or with special needs, with the result that offenders with these difficulties were either inappropriately assessed or missed out on programmes. Part of the difficulty lay in the reliance on written work and the requirement for homework. Problem-solving skills programmes were also seen to require a certain level of theoretical comprehension. One manager called for an adapted ETS: 'I see men who would be better equipped to undertake an SOTP if they had done an adapted ETS first. If you look at some of the deficits that SOTP people might have, such as being anti-social, lacking social skills like supporting each other, which they need to develop before they undertake the work..'

Specific enquiries were made about how the Canadian and Scottish panels address issues of diversity, and advice was sought from Ellie Scrivens as to relevant developments in health care accreditation. It does not seem that these issues have been taken further in those other settings. In the health setting, a recent development has been the inclusion of consumer representation in the accreditation process, either in the writing of standards or in the review process. According to Ellie Scrivens, very similar issues arose in health to the ones discussed above. Including the consumer perspective raised the question whether to bring in one consumer to represent the whole of the relevant population, someone representing a consumer organisation, or an 'expert' consumer. In relation to standards, the question was whether to have special 'diversity' standards or to seek to ensure that all standards recognise diversity in the population.

According to information received, the Scottish Panel, consisting of a majority of women, shows particular concern for female prisoners, specifically monitoring the suitability of the Scottish Anger Management Programme. Ethnicity is not seen as an acute issue in Scotland, where there are only 80 ethnic minority prisoners in the entire Scottish prison estate, but the Scottish Prison Service is said to have well-articulated policies on ethnic minorities. In Canada, by contrast, ethnic minority issues have a high profile, given the existence of sizeable indigenous population groups. The Canadian Panel requires applicants for accreditation to address the question of diversity, and their aim is to recruit as diversified a group of panel members as possible.

Panel costs

One complex area of inquiry was the cost of the accreditation process. Here, the terms of reference did not require a full economic appraisal of the Panel involving a cost benefit analysis. In assessing costs, the difficulty lay in drawing the line between the contribution that JAP makes to the wider 'What Works' enterprise within the prison and probation services, and the support that the latter agencies provide to enable JAP to fulfil its specific remit. Following consultation with the Steering Group, the following costs were examined:

- *Direct costs of the JAP and its secretariat*, as provided in budget statements supplied by the secretariat. To this we re-added the costs of the secretariat, letter writers and the commitment given by nominated and co-opted members of JAP. These costs were calculated for 2001/02 as the most recent full financial year, providing an indication of the costs of the Panel in 'normal operation'. As well as providing an overall cost for the financial year, a cost per Panel Day was estimated including the daily fee for appointed Panel members, the day costs of participation by nominated members and other personnel including the secretariat and letter writers, and an element for accommodation.

- *Programme submission costs* – based on questions asked during interviews with programme developers, NPD and OBPU, plus additional enquiries where necessary, an assessment was made of the costs of a 'typical' submission to JAP, taking account of the length of the submission process. Here, we re-estimated both the local costs (such as preparing submission documents, responding to panel comments and meeting its requirements) and the costs of the headquarters element in providing advice and support for the submission up to the point of application. To that we added an estimate of the direct JAP costs, based on the amount of time committed by the Panel to consideration of the submission.

Unavoidably, this could only provide estimates of costs, but these are perhaps sufficient for judgements about the value for money that the Panel offers. The following conclusions were drawn from our calculations:

- The direct costs of the Panel had remained reasonably stable over the period of its operation so far. Official expenditure in 2001/02, at £231,396, was slightly higher than in 2000/01 (£202,978) but included the costs of the evaluation (1999/2000 was not a full year of operation). Projected expenditure for 2002/03 at £369,460 included £150,000 for recruitment/contingency without which it would be slightly below expenditure for 2001/02. What is not apparent here is any escalation in the costs of the Panel.

- Direct costs totalling £371,376 in 2001/02 were identified, covering the costs of the secretariat (£48,301), letter writers (£6,950) and commitments by ex-officio members or participants (£84,729). In fact, secretariat costs were below what might be regarded as its full complement. As from January 2002, the secretariat comprised one full time SEO, 0.5 HEO and 0.5 EO, which in 2001/02 would have cost £59,732 over the full year.

- The costs of a Panel Day were estimated at £14,248, covering the cost of the personnel listed above, plus accommodation. It was not possible to allocate a cost for travel and subsistence. Although official expenditure on travel and subsistence was over £27,000 in 2001/02, this is presumed to include travel other than to attend Panel meetings but not necessarily *all* travel to Panel meetings (i.e. some attendance may have been funded from other sources). It is useful to note, however, that the 'people' costs of assembling the Panel and providing secretariat and letter writing cover were a little below £10,000 per day in 2001/02.

● The costs of getting a typical 'in-service' programme accredited by the Panel (involving two submissions) varied between £25,000 to £30,000. On the basis of somewhat limited information, repeated submissions to the Panel appeared to increase costs for all participants (in other words, more staff time in preparation did not necessarily save Panel costs).

Compared with the overall budget of the prison and probation services, the costs of accreditation must be counted as small.[15] Only time will tell whether accreditation has been cost-effective in helping the Services to achieve their target of reducing reconviction by five per cent under Aim 4 of the Home Office Correctional Policy Framework, as evidence from evaluations of accredited programmes is only beginning to emerge.[16] It would be misleading to compare the above costs with those arising from the activities of the Panels in Scotland and Canada in the absence of a similarly detailed analysis of cost in those other two jurisdictions. However, various options for changing the way the Panel runs might have marginal cost implications, though a reduced cost in one area will often be balanced by an increased cost elsewhere. The cost implications of different options are indicated below:

1. Changes in Panel membership (to be reduced from 20 to 16 including Sir Duncan Nichol and three ex-officio members); however, others are likely to continue to attend in an advisory capacity, so significant costs savings are unlikely.

2. Running more sub panels (the Canadian model). In cost terms, unlikely to differ from the current arrangement, effectively a number of sub panels meeting within the same week (there might be savings if the need to consider a particular type of programme ceases).

3. Additional Panel time – the suggestion that the Panel might meet for an extra week or a portion thereof (each extra day would cost £10,000 for the personnel including Panel members' fees).

---

15 According to the New Choreography (National Probation Service, 2001), Probation Service expenditure for 2001/2 was £640 million. Prison Service costs exceeded £2,000 million (HM Prison Service, 2002).

16 Friendship et al., (2002) report reduced reconviction following participation in pre-accreditation cognitive skills programmes in prison, a finding that was not repeated in the subsequent study of accredited programmes by Falshaw et al, (2003). Hollin et al., (2002) reports encouraging initial findings on implementing pathfinder probation programmes. However, it is understood that a retrospective reconviction study by Oxford University of Think First probation pathfinder projects shows disappointing results – see note 5 above. Results were presented at What Works Conference 2002, and at the time of writing await publication. A prospective study is so far finding positive treatment effects.

4. Preview time/Accrediting programmes 'on site' by previewer(s) or small panel – (additional fees for previewing members, offset against Panel and letter writing time in formal session).

5. Material presented other than in writing, e.g. videos, presentation by programme development/implementation managers (less Panel time required for reading, additional costs in submission preparation).

6. Delegating some functions, e.g. to the secretariat or a 'shepherd' (shepherd's fees offset against Panel and letter writing time in formal session).

7. Decisions by correspondence or e-mail rather than in meetings (reduced requirement for Panel time, additional fees/costs for reading material and commenting outside panel meetings).

Conclusions and recommendations

Both Panel members and programme developers described the Panel as adopting a constructive collaborative approach in considering programme submissions, and there was a consensus in favour of high standards to maintain the effectiveness and credibility of accredited programmes. The sheer volume of submission material presented difficulties for Panel members, yet programme developers were understandably frustrated if they thought insufficient attention had been given to the fruits of their hard work. Generally programme developers identified a need for clearer guidance on the requirements and expectations of the Panel, closer liaison with Panel members and clearer feedback on whether recommended changes to submission material were mandatory rather than desirable. To some extent, the publication of audit performance standards for probation programmes will have clarified the requirements (see: Joint Prison/Probation Services Accreditation Panel, HMI Probation, and National Probation Service, 2002). Another issue was the gatekeeping role played by Prison and Probation Headquarters; though necessary, this was seen as potentially constraining, and as disadvantaging non-prison or probation programme developers who might not be in a position to commission the expertise and research needed for a convincing application.

The question of diversity was prominent in the data collection, and this area has been the subject of a variety of recent initiatives: the appointment of a diversity advisor to the Panel, the Prisons/Probation Diversity Review, and research on the literacy requirements for offenders attending accredited programmes and on the criminogenic needs of black and Asian offenders. Indeed, its new terms of reference charge the Panel with ensuring that diversity issues are taken into account in programme development, accreditation and implementation. This will give the Panel scope to take a more proactive stance in promoting steps to address diversity, perhaps through encouraging pilot work to explore how interventions can cater for the needs of ethnic minorities, women and offenders who lack basic skills.

The following recommendations are intended to refine the submission process, and enhance its legitimacy by increasing the extent to which it demonstrably offers a level playing field:

Fourth recommendation: Provide clearer guidance on the structure of programme submissions and the contents of the different manuals. Consider introducing pro-forma manuals, or where this is inappropriate provide examples of material that has previously been found helpful. Consider how Panel feedback might make a clearer distinction between adjustments that are required before accreditation can be achieved as opposed to changes that are desirable.

Fifth recommendation: Appoint panel members as previewers of programme submissions to brief and guide sub panel discussion. Consider site visits by previewer(s) to liaise with programme developers about Panel requirements, and observe delivery of programme. Consider arrangements to ensure that the previewer does not commit the Panel to a particular decision, for example by not chairing the sub panel considering the submission.

Sixth recommendation: Consider submission of non-paper material, for example videos, presentations by programme developers or implementation managers, electronic format (CD roms).

5.   Other contributions to 'What Works'

This chapter starts with the broader question of how far a culture of effective practice seems to have developed within the prison and probation services, drawing largely on the survey and interviews with programme staff. It then looks at sentencers' understanding of accredited programmes. Having considered some of the challenges presented in implementing accredited programmes, the chapter reviews the role of the Panel in curriculum development and in setting audit requirements.

Prison and probation: a culture of effectiveness?

One of the first points to emerge from the survey of programme staff is that this workforce saw itself as having a good knowledge of 'What Works' (over 80% saw themselves as having detailed knowledge, or at least a reasonable overview). Perhaps it is not surprising that managers generally regarded themselves as more knowledgeable about 'What Works' than did tutors (the eight people who admitted to no knowledge of the literature all being tutors). Of course, levels of knowledge amongst programme staff cannot be attributed directly to JAP's work, though it is doubtless due to the climate in which JAP operates and which it influences. The other encouraging finding for those sponsoring the Panel is the overwhelming agreement with the emphasis on programme design being aimed at reducing offending (well over 90% of the sample). A substantial minority – 14 per cent – took issue with the use of reconviction rates as a measure of success, mainly because conviction was not seen as an accurate measure of offending or because other measures of improvement (employment, housing, and drugs use) were seen as equally important. But this apart, these results offer a clear endorsement by programme staff of the overall project to which JAP is contributing.

Knowledge of the Panel's activities

The vast majority of programme staff said they had heard of JAP, almost all the managers and 70 per cent of the tutors (a finding that may surprise Panel members and policy administrators, who expected a lower level of awareness). Colleagues were most commonly cited as a source of information, particularly by tutors (ticked by 70% of the tutors who had heard of the Panel or its Prison Service predecessors). Both line managers and strategic managers seemed more likely than tutors to obtain information about JAP from training, and strategic managers seemed significantly more likely to draw from conference presentations, professional journals, and probation circulars (all mentioned by around a fifth of tutors). This does suggest that tutors are mostly hearing about the Panel informally, and that it might be worth investing more effort into relaying more systematic or written information to that staff group.

The small proportion of prison personal officers who responded to the survey also showed a high level of awareness of 'What Works' research (77% having at least some knowledge, although relatively few saw themselves as having detailed knowledge). Two-thirds agreed with the emphasis on reducing offending, although less than half (45%) supported the use of reconviction rates as a measure of programme effectiveness. Knowledge of JAP was far more limited amongst personal officers than amongst programme staff, with over 70 per cent having not heard of the Panel or having no knowledge about its decisions. However, they did see themselves as quite well-informed about local programmes for offenders, they found that information useful, and they said that it influenced their decisions about prisoners (though there were large numbers in the 'middling' category in response to both questions). Here, colleagues seemed by far the most common source of information, and relatively few seemed to access sources of information outside their immediate work environment. Where they did gain access to such information, it was mainly Home Office reports, professional journals or conference presentations.

Sources of information about the Panel

In interview, a number of members of programme staff thought that the information they received about the Panel's activities was adequate for their purposes, that sources of information were accessible and that headquarters personnel were approachable and helpful. Useful sources of information included: the Panel's 2nd Annual Report (internet); a glossy headquarters summary of Panel membership and activities; a Panel member's visit; presentations from headquarters managers or JAP members at conferences or training events; and audit feedback. However, despite efforts to brief staff, the more common view was that information was inadequate or lacking, or negative in tone. Little information was seen to be provided directly to those running programmes, and it was apparently not filtered down from senior manager meetings (either to or via middle managers). Programme staff did not see themselves as well-informed about the evidence underlying accredited programmes, nor about new programmes being developed or piloted. Although this might not be JAP's direct responsibility, it was seen by programme staff as impinging upon the credibility of the Panel's work (and their ability to persuade colleagues of the value of accredited programmes). A number of people recognised, however, that the problem was not necessarily simply a lack of information: in-service information flows did not always operate well, and it was difficult to provide information in a form that busy people would find time to read.

Amongst the types of information that programme managers and staff thought might be useful for the future were the following:

- An information pack containing briefing notes and guides as a resource for programme/treatment managers to use with tutors or non-programme staff.

- Videos and booklets. Bulletins with clear straightforward information about evidence or research results. Material, circulated directly to tutors, which could be used with non-programme colleagues or with offenders who query their attendance on a programme.

- Discussion with colleagues in which there was a chance to reflect, share ideas and learn from each other (the evaluation was seen as providing an opportunity for this kind of process); regular updates at programme unit meetings.

- A help line for queries about programme materials or delivery, particularly when a new programme was being implemented; a contact person at headquarters who could provide practical advice to treatment managers.

- A 'news' section on NPD web site, intranet, internet discussion group, using the e-mail to canvass views on programme changes; an online reference manual for each programme.

- Input on JAP, and their role in the accreditation process, in annual training for treatment managers, and in tutor training on individual programmes.

A communications strategy

Support can be drawn from the above discussion for stronger lines of communication between the Panel and practice, and a communications strategy, a need identified alike by JAP interviewees and programme developers. One Panel member suggested that ownership needed to be promoted by giving credit to others – tutors, treatment and programme managers, and senior managers – who had played a role in developing effective practice.

Panel members were keen to understand the problems and constraints faced by staff in delivering accredited programmes and where they perceived a need to deviate from programme manuals. Some proposed that programme staff should have an opportunity to transmit written concerns about an aspect of a programme, or an exercise, direct to the Panel. Indeed, an opportunity for problems to be reported back to JAP will be provided by the 'Change Control System' developed by NPD and approved by JAP in September 2002 for launch over Autumn 2002. Under this system, the Joint Change Control Panel (comprising Panel members amongst others) will receive reports from NPD and Prison Service Headquarters and submit an annual report to JAP proposing possible changes in both prisons and probation programmes. The processes by which issues reach the Change Control Panel appear to differ between the two agencies, however, in that arrangements in the NPD build upon its existing infra-structure of regional 'What Works' managers, who will collect feedback from the field to relay to NPD. This is a structure that the Prison Service lacks, and feedback there will come from prison treatment managers to Headquarters staff.

Programme staff were asked on the questionnaire to describe JAP's role in their own words, rather than to select from pre-coded categories. Over 40 per cent of respondents (over half of managers) saw that role as what is categorised here as 'quality control' (maintaining standards, evaluating programme quality), and over a quarter referred to the Panel as an 'overseer' (determining which programmes are to be used, and criteria applied). It is perhaps disappointing that fewer respondents mentioned 'programme design' (development and advice on content and delivery), and only five per cent (mostly strategic managers) highlighted a research element.

Actual knowledge of the decisions made by JAP was less common, and illustrations of detailed knowledge seemed to relate to programmes (mainly sex offender treatment or cognitive behavioural) rather than Panel decisions. The majority of tutors saw themselves as having only some knowledge, or none at all, and only 39 respondents (24%) claimed a detailed knowledge or reasonable overview.

These views suggest that an awareness of JAP, and some aspects of its role, has impinged on practitioners, but it does not amount to an in-depth understanding of the Panel's decisions or what informs these. Based on their responses to the survey, programme staff seemed to perceive some of the achievements identified by Panel members in interview, such as promoting rigour and the development of a strong set of validated programmes. However, there seemed greater awareness of the controlling rather than the developmental aspects of the Panel's work, and limited appreciation of the emphasis on research. This leaves scope to raise practitioners' awareness of these wider activities.

Sentencers' understanding of effectiveness

The sentencer perspective is important, as the sentencing decision dictates, in part, whether an offender has access to an offending behaviour programme. During the surveying and interviewing process judges and magistrates, were asked about their level of knowledge of offender programmes, and their sources of information. They were also asked what additional information they might find helpful, and how this might influence a sentencing decision. Their responses revealed a strong case for the provision of good quality, accessible information about accredited programmes to sentencers, and that this would be likely to increase their confidence in community-based programmes for offenders and therefore their choice of such programmes instead of custody. The response rate to the survey, at 46 per cent, was lower than that secured for programme staff (see Chapter 2), and the views summarised below may therefore overstate the level of knowledge amongst sentencers (on the assumption that those who had not heard of the Panel might have been less inclined to complete the questionnaire). Nevertheless, the data remain very interesting.

There was some awareness of the effective practice initiative amongst the sentencers who responded to the survey. Around half saw themselves as reasonably well-informed about the effectiveness of offender programmes, and just under half had heard of JAP. They seemed to have a similar understanding of JAP's function to programme staff, with the majority identifying the Panel's role as monitoring effectiveness and ensuring high quality programmes. Nearly half also perceived a research element – either conducting research or ensuring programmes are based on evidence. Interviewees saw the validating or quality assurance role as significant in giving sentencers confidence in the integrity of programmes for offenders as endorsed by a body outside the Probation Service.

Sentencers from all areas certainly believed themselves to be well-informed about programmes available locally as well as accredited programmes – two-thirds saying in questionnaires that they had received at least some information about offender programmes. Interviewees revealed very variable levels of knowledge about accreditation, and little awareness of the research background, but saw themselves as very well-informed about local programmes. The Probation Service was seen as the main source of information, both through pre-sentence reports (PSRs) and through other forms of liaison between senior managers and courts, and the downgrading of probation liaison committees was a source of regret to magistrates. Court circulars and training were other important sources of information, particularly for magistrates. Both surveyed and interviewed sentencers clearly wanted more information about programme effectiveness, and interviewees stressed the need for good quality timely information. Most survey respondents found information about accredited and local programmes quite or very useful, and almost all indicated that it influenced their sentencing decisions at least to some extent.

Sentencers, especially judges, were explicit about how information about accredited programmes might influence their sentencing decision – in favour of a community sentence where an offence was at the threshold between community and custody. Considerable confidence was expressed in PSRs, and sentencers portrayed themselves as reluctant to go against a realistic proposal for a community option (usually equating programmes with a community sentence). There is clearly scope here to inform sentencers about accreditation and about accredited programmes. Although detailed technical information did not seem to be desirable, sentencers were interested in knowing that a programme was likely to work. There were useful suggestions for how that information might be provided, and examples were given of information that sentencers had previously found useful in related contexts:

- Loose-leaf booklet in the Retiring Room, with information about the content of programmes and what has been found to work. Regularly updated.

- Videos, bulletins, lunchtime presentations.

- Direct contact with staff delivering programmes, and visits to programmes.

- Leaflet or summary of programme attached to PSRs.

- E-mail summaries of new programme content.

- Information published in *The Magistrate*, or by HM Probation Inspectorate.

Implementing effective programmes: the challenges

Crucial to the development of a culture of effective practice in the prison and probation services is the successful implementation of programmes as accredited by the Panel, so that their worth becomes apparent to other colleagues. Here, stakeholders were aware of real challenges, as we consider in this section.

Maintaining programme integrity

JAP members were aware of numerous obstacles to the widespread achievement of effective programmes for offenders, and seemed quite troubled by some of these issues. Of major concern was how to ensure that programmes were delivered as intended, perhaps in a variety of locations, so that they achieved the desired aims.[17] Questions troubling Panel members included whether the accreditation process had perhaps produced programmes that were too complex for general 'roll out': might programmes look fine on paper, but prove difficult to operate in practice? Were the resources – specifically staff skills and training – adequate to ensure the maintenance of quality as programmes were translated to new settings, and detached from their original conceptualisation and design? One suggestion at the academic seminar was that greater use could be made of literature on effective implementation (such as Bernfeld *et al.*, 2001 and Gendreau *et al.*, 1999).

Speed of implementation, coupled with wider recruitment problems, was seen as a major issue for the Probation Service in ensuring that staff members were adequately prepared for accredited programmes, and it was suggested that what was needed now was a period of consolidation rather than the production of new programmes. Although its lengthier experience of accredited programmes had enabled the Prison Service to develop staff skills in the area of treatment management and audit, geographical constraints were seen to affect its ability to recruit staff of the right calibre to deliver programmes. Programme development was seen as requiring specialised skills, which both services needed to nurture.

For their part, programme staff clearly saw accredited programmes as effective, and tutors cited examples of individual offenders whom they saw as having been changed by the experience of going through a programme. Some tutors described themselves as having confidence in delivering a programme because they knew it had been accredited, and accreditation was seen as securing credibility with managers and other colleagues, and also with offenders. Perceptions of the effectiveness of accredited programmes improved job satisfaction, as staff perceived that they were making a difference and saw the training for accredited programmes as an investment in them as valued practitioners. Prison officers appeared to find their jobs more interesting as a result of developing tutoring skills, which they saw as enhancing other aspects of their performance. However, the psychological language and structured style of some programmes was experienced as de-skilling to tutors, particularly by some probation staff. For the latter, the

---

17 There are analogous issues in the more general field of crime prevention, on which see, for example, Crawford (1998, ch. 5). As Crawford points out, 'only belatedly have issues concerned with the implementation and delivery of crime prevention [programmes] risen to the fore' in the research literature in that field (p.161), despite early and striking research results (for example, Hope and Murphy, 1983) pointing to the potential importance of 'implementation failure' in contributing to disappointing programme results.

transition to nationally developed programmes had created some loss of 'ownership' of programmes traditionally developed locally, and a sense that traditional practitioner expertise in engaging offenders was not valued by those making decisions centrally about the implementation of programmes. A small number of interviewees also commented that the content of programmes made delivery, or engaging offenders, difficult, for the following reasons:

- *Language used in programmes.* Some tutors found that difficulties in understanding the material diminished their ability to deliver it successfully (e.g. TF and ETS). The psychological style of the language of accredited programmes was seen to arise from the skew in JAP membership towards psychologists.

- *Programme material.* Some of the sessions in TF were described as dry, boring, and like school lessons. Especially when they appeared at the beginning of programmes, such sessions were seen as undermining attendance (TF was also the target of a number of negative questionnaire comments for being patronising, poorly written and difficult to present). More practical sessions were seen as more successful in engaging offenders than more theoretical material that was difficult to apply to practical situations. The theoretical nature of some material had led some tutors to see JAP as detached from practice.

- *Quality of programme manual.* The TF manual was not seen as giving clear guidelines to tutors – language was seen as obscure, and the structure criticised. Lack of clarity might lead to different interpretations of what was required and consequent loss of treatment integrity. This was contrasted with experience of the Drink Impaired Drivers (DIDS) manual, which was regarded as simple and easy to follow.

An absence of advice was perceived about the circumstances in which programme material could be adjusted, on an on-site basis, to accommodate different learning styles and to foster engagement. Interviewees described fairly negative experiences of seeking advice from Headquarters, encountering what they saw as rigid attitudes, and a lack of appreciation of the practicalities of delivery (in the Prison Service), or simply the absence of a mechanism by which advice could be sought or modifications proposed (Probation Service). This resulted in some disillusionment, and a perception that their views were not listened to or valued; the Panel was sometimes wrongly perceived as the source of control. The introduction of the Change Control System, as discussed above, is clearly an attempt to enable practitioners' views as well as evaluation findings to reach the Panel, and it remains to be seen whether this will give practitioners confidence that their voices are being heard.

A specific dilemma that was identified concerned the need to secure programme integrity whilst simultaneously ensuring that programmes were responsive to the needs of different groups and individuals (what might be seen as treatment integrity). In view of the interest shown by JAP members in practitioners' views about the circumstances requiring them to deviate from the programme manual, we incorporated a question on this point in our interviews with programme staff. Generally, SOTP and Cognitive Self Change were seen as more flexible and responsive to offenders' needs than were ETS or TF. A small minority of programme staff (8) endorsed the need to stick closely to the manual; most of these worked in the Prison Service, where a little more faith was expressed that methods of delivery were based on evaluation. Reasons cited for adherence to manual requirements included: to avoid loss of audit points; to ensure consistency – and equality of treatment – across different sites; to enable programmes to be evaluated; and to ensure relatively inexperienced staff delivered to an acceptable standard.

The most commonly given reason for deviating from the programme manual was the need to respond to the individual needs and characteristics of offenders. Twenty interviewees referred to an apparent contradiction between the need to be responsive and a requirement to deliver as prescribed (SOTP and One-to-One were seen as giving considerable scope for responsivity). A variety of circumstances were cited as creating a need for some flexibility: to accommodate diversity and learning styles; speeding up or slowing down the pace to match the learning of the group; making the programme material 'real' or using more realistic, relevant examples; dealing with important issues that cannot be predicted or ignored (e.g. where an offender achieves an important breakthrough in understanding). The optimal position was regarded as one which allowed some personalisation of delivery without losing programme structure or treatment objectives. Experience, and the development of appropriate skills, was seen as a prerequisite for making the relevant judgements, and the role of the treatment manager in maintaining treatment integrity through supervision was seen as crucial.

Management support, both at the local and at the agency or organisational level, was seen as critical to the maintenance of effective programmes. Panel members perceived a possibility that the delivery of a programme within a prison might be undermined by the absence of the governor's support, or that an agency might regard itself as having had enough advice from 'the experts' and overlook the need for continued Panel input. Other dangers were envisaged: for example, the impetus might be lost if times became more financially constrained; or senior managers might dispute the 'What Works' philosophy, regarding their job as being to ensure security or containment rather than constructive work with prisoners. In both prison and probation services, there was some perception that accredited programmes diverted resources from other important work with offenders; for example, some thought that a disproportionate effort was being put into work with more interesting or challenging offenders (such as sex offenders). Doubts about the level of organisational support for programmes were reinforced by the experiences recounted by some programme staff, who saw case managers as having a crucial role in reinforcing the value of programmatic work. The prison regime and environment was not always seen as supportive, with practical constraints and a lack of awareness of programmes being cited as creating particular difficulties.

Programme completion rates

Difficulties in getting offenders through programmes, especially community-based programmes, were raised by a number of interviewees as a factor impeding programme success. Poor attendance was attributed to various factors: required psychometric tests were off-putting to offenders; case management needed to be strengthened; and there was a failure to engage offenders actively in the process of change. The issue of responsivity received considerable attention from all groups of respondents; for example, how some practitioners were able to use programme material effectively with offenders was identified at the academic seminar as a potential area for research. As the NPD recognised in its response to the Interim Report, different challenges were presented in the prison and probation settings: probation work has to compete with other attractions in offenders' lives, whereas prison-based programmes have to compete with other institutional priorities.

For the purposes of assessing agency performance against Key Performance Indicator (KPI) targets, the number of offenders actually completing a specific programme is multiplied by the percentage IQR (Implementation Quality Rating) score awarded by the audit process (see below) for the quality of delivery at that site. According to official records obtained from OBPU, on this basis the Prison Service achieved 6405 completions in 2001/02, taking account of IQR scores averaging 95 per cent (meaning that 95% of actual completions were counted). 839 of these completions were of SOTP. This compared with 5986 KPI completions in 2000/01 (786 for SOTP) – see HM Prison Service (2001). The Prison Service thus exceeded its KPI targets in both years for all programmes (the targets were 5000 in 2000/01 and 6100 in 2001/02). It did not, however, achieve its SOTP targets; instead reaching 77 per cent of its SOTP target in 2000/01 (target=1020) and 72 per cent in 2001/02 (target=1160).

The National Probation Service's Accredited Programmes Performance Report 2001-02, obtained from NPD, shows that 3431 actual completions were achieved for the year, as against a target of 6267 (a 55% success rate). Multiplied by an average IQR score of 70 per cent, the 'KPI' completions then constituted only 38 per cent of the target figure. This is considerably below the Prison Service KPI figure, a contrast discussed further below. On the positive side, the targets for getting offenders referred to accredited programmes for the year were slightly exceeded, and the proportion of orders and licences with a requirement to attend an accredited programme was 77 per cent of the expected figure. But these data relate to referrals or requirements, not completions. One important factor associated with the disappointing net completion rate could have been that selection was poor: risk profiles did not meet targets, with both low and high risk offenders being over-represented and medium risk offenders being under-represented. However, the real problem appeared to lie with offenders dropping out before they started or during programmes, with only around half the orders made resulting in programme 'starts'. Relevant factors here were cited as case management, delivery capacity, time to programme start and motivation. The Panel was briefed about these issues at its meeting in February/March 2002, as an aspect of the operational environment about which it would wish to be aware. This sort of information is clearly useful to the Panel in considering the practical constraints of delivery.[18]

Curriculum development – advice to applicants

It seems clear that JAP's main contributions to a curriculum of effective programmes took the form of its standard-setting for accreditation and advice and feedback, especially in helping to develop programmes submitted for advice. The Panel was not seen as having much opportunity to play a significant role in decisions about programme development, except in response to individual submissions in an area that was seen as under-developed. Generally, programme development was regarded as the responsibility of the sponsoring agencies. The piloting of new approaches (under the probation Pathfinder initiative) was seen as the prison and probation services' rather than the Panel's remit, although the latter might have a role in reviewing whether accredited programmes met the range of dynamic risk factors.

Reference has already been made to the value that Panel members placed on providing feedback to programme developers during the submission process, and the direct dialogue with applicants. In the past, those submitting programmes for advice were allowed to attend the Panel hearing to hear directly from Panel members. Some Panel members described subsequent visits to programme sites to explain written advice in more detail, clarify misunderstandings and help identify ways forward. Much of this contact was mediated

---

18 See Underdown (2001) for a discussion of the challenge facing the 'What Works' initiative to improving on past probation service performance on attendance and completion rates.

through OBPU and DSU (both within the Prison Service Sentence Management Group) and NPD staff. Panel members clearly appreciated hearing that their advice had been helpful and seeing the resulting improvements in programmes as they moved towards accreditation (such experiences featured strongly in Panel members' accounts of 'rewarding' experiences of accrediting programmes). On the other hand, some experiences of providing feedback were depicted as demanding and challenging, particularly when submissions were seen to fall far short of the required standard. This factor seems to have caused a change of the Panel's policy, so that applicants for accreditation (as opposed to for advice) were no longer required to attend Panel.

Programme developers clearly appreciated direct and specific feedback from the Panel (as mentioned above) and wanted more of it. Overall, despite some painful experiences, developers valued attending Panel meetings, particularly where representatives of a sub panel had time to give direct feedback. One or two more experienced programme developers described wanting more active engagement with the Panel. One recounted having to be persistent in seeking answers to questions that the Panel might not have fully addressed, and another expressed frustration at a perceived inability to involve Panel members in discussions about further development of accredited programmes.

Of the programme staff who responded to the survey, only 39 (24%), and just 15 per cent of tutors, were aware of advice from the Panel having been given on a programme on which they were working – and only 10 per cent or fewer respondents from Nottinghamshire and Greater Manchester probation areas. Where advice was referred to, it was viewed positively, with 49 per cent rating it as useful or very useful, and 46 per cent as fair or very fair (18% found the advice of little or no use, and 10% quite or very unfair). There is some support here for the perceptions conveyed by panel members of 'adding value' in commenting and making recommendations regarding individual programmes.

Experiences of audit

The arrangements for auditing the management and delivery of accredited programmes are intended to ensure that programmes are implemented as approved by the Panel. The audit of prison programmes is the responsibility of OBPU, using criteria developed as part of the documentation for the programme in question. Probation programmes are audited by HM Probation Inspectorate, using the Performance Standards Manual 2002 to produce IQR scores based on four aspects of programme implementation: committed leadership and supportive management (20% of total marks); programme management responsibilities

(30%); quality of programme delivery (30%); and case management responsibilities (20%). Having these requirements specified in a common manual means they are available to inform programme submissions; this may alleviate some of the problems of implementation discussed above.

Interviewees saw audit as a powerful tool, for example in ensuring that programmes received the necessary commitment and resources. The stronger emphasis recently given by JAP to audit arrangements and reports was welcomed, despite some scepticism about the measurement of 'quality', and scepticism also about the pressures on auditors to ensure that programmes passed. The Panel was seen (by those who discussed the matter) as having an oversight role in approving the documents against which programmes were audited, and also in considering audit findings. However, checking programmes against the audit criteria was seen as the proper responsibility of the correctional agencies. Here, an issue of concern for some interviewees was the disparity between the arrangements for audit in the prison and probation services, particularly the fact that audit remained the responsibility of OBPU in the Prison Service. It was thought by these respondents that the prison audit function should be separated from the sponsoring/gatekeeping function, which OBPU also carries. As one interviewee put it, it was difficult for the unit to be managing and supporting programme and treatment staff most of the time, then to act as an objective judge of their performance in an audit. In recognition of these concerns, the Panel was encouraging the Services to move towards a unified system of audit, and attempts were being made to rationalise audit arrangements in the Prison Service under an audit development sub-group established by the What Works in Prison Strategy Board. The adoption of a model similar to probation audit arrangements – that is, the audit function being undertaken by the relevant Inspectorate – had been resisted by HM Inspectorate of Prisons, which did not see the audit of accredited programmes as falling within its statutory terms of reference.

Some interviewees also commented on the contrast in IQR scores awarded in audit by OBPU on the one hand, and the Probation Inspectorate on the other (see above). They suspected that such differences were more likely to reflect differences in audit criteria than differences in the respective quality of prison and probation delivery. In contrast to prison establishment scores usually exceeding 90 per cent, none of the first 15 probation areas whose audit reports were published by the end of March 2002 achieved IQR scores above 70 per cent (see: HMI Probation, 2002). The superficial impression is that tougher standards are being applied to the Probation Service than to the Prison Service, with implications for each service's ability to reach KPI targets, a matter of proper concern to the Panel.

Despite these variations, programme staff reported positive experiences of the process of being audited (see: Appendix II). Of those who had direct experience of being audited, staff predominantly regarded the process as useful and fair (72% as very or quite useful, and 74% as very or quite fair), though prison staff rated audit findings more highly than did probation staff. Additional comments, where given, supported these ratings. Usually, staff seemed to view the audit as fair and constructive in helping them to improve their practice. There were, however, some concerns about judgements being subjective, or not focused sufficiently on questions of quality. Some tutors seemed to find the experience stressful and time consuming, but – as a group – they remained able to perceive benefits for their practice in terms of keeping programmes focused or achieving standards. One interesting point related to a perceived lack of consultation between auditors and those delivering programmes about the day-to-day problems influencing programme integrity.

Conclusions and recommendations

The news from programme staff is encouraging, with a clear endorsement of the 'What Works' project, a strong commitment to accredited programmes and a reasonable understanding of the role performed by the Panel (though limited awareness of the research input). However, interviewed programme staff saw their information about the Panel's activities as inadequate. This impinged on their faith in accredited programmes, as did their perception of a poor response from Headquarters (taken as evidence of a 'controlling' stance by the Panel) to requests for advice about or proposed modifications to programme content or delivery. There were signs that in the long run this could damage the Panel's legitimacy and the credibility of its decisions.

Although sentencers saw themselves as reasonably informed about programme effectiveness and accredited programmes (especially programmes available locally), there was clearly an appetite for more information about effectiveness, and a belief that this would enhance confidence in community-based programmes. They wanted this information to be of good quality, timely, and accessible so that it could inform sentencing decisions. Briefing sentencers is clearly the primary responsibility of the correctional services, but it may well be that JAP could play a role, as did Professor Don Grubin (a Panel member) in the video for sentencers 'An Insight into What Works', produced by the NPD in September 2002.

There is ample support from the research evidence for the development of a stronger communications strategy, a need identified by both JAP interviewees and programme developers. Indeed, a programme tutor and a magistrate both independently commented on their difficulties in locating the Panel's 2nd Report on the National Probation Service web site. The revised terms of reference for the Panel recognise the need to raise its profile with staff in the correctional services, a point reinforced by the low response rate to our survey of prison personal officers and probation PSR authors and case managers. This poor response could reflect a lack of engagement with accredited programmes on the part of staff upon whose active support the success of the 'What Works' initiative depends (the National Probation Service's Accredited Programmes Performance Report 2001-02 highlighting the importance of case management and motivational work with offenders). The survey of sentencers also indicates that it would be worth taking their needs (at least for information about accredited programmes, if not directly about the activities of the Panel) into account in developing the Panel's communications strategy.

Views from programme staff underline the need for an adequate change control mechanism to demonstrate that their concerns about specific programme materials are taken seriously, and transmitted appropriately to the Panel to inform its review of accredited programmes. The authors of this report are aware that a joint change control mechanism has been launched, and fully endorse this development. Ideally, a balance can be found between allowing the Panel to learn directly from practitioners and ensuring reasonable stability and certainty in programme content. Another area where there is scope to strengthen the Panel's role, whilst leaving the primary responsibility for programme development and implementation with the correctional services, is curriculum development and the piloting of new approaches (particularly those that address issues of diversity). Again, this has been recognised in the revised terms of reference for the Panel, which give it the remit to advise the correctional services on curriculum development on the basis of an annual review of developments in research. Given the range of views encountered on diversity (see also Chapter 4) and on programme integrity and responsivity, the Panel could both raise its own profile and engage in useful two-way debates on these questions with programme developers and practitioners by organising or participating in seminars on specific topics.

Given the growing importance of the audit function in assuring quality in the delivery of accredited programmes, there is also a need to ensure that prison and probation audit arrangements are independent and equitable. This report fully supports the Panel's stance in encouraging the development of unified audit arrangements for the correctional services. Until such time as this is achieved, it is strongly suggested that the audit function should not rest with the main sponsoring/gatekeeping unit (OBPU) in the Prison Service. To preserve the credibility of audit in assuring that programmes are implemented as approved by the Panel, that function should not remain within the Prison Service Sentence Management Group.

Seventh recommendation: In order to increase the Panel's visibility and the transparency of its decisions, there is a need for a strategic approach to communication between the Panel and staff in the correctional services on a range of issues. There is also a need to ensure that the Panel plays an appropriate role in informing sentencers about programme effectiveness. Consider the following mechanisms: intranet, internet, and e-mail; information

pack distributed to treatment managers; accessible booklets for sentencers regularly updated; panel members to visit programme sites, and contribute to conferences and training events; seminars with programme staff to debate important issues e.g. diversity, models of change for women, programme integrity, responsivity.

Eighth recommendation: Pending the introduction of a unified system of audit for the correctional services, a body outside the Prison Service Sentence Management Group should undertake the audit function.

6.   Future directions

The findings presented in this report show that the Panel can claim significant achievements in the period since it was established. Its main achievement lies in the accreditation of high quality programmes, and in the provision of advice to programme developers contributing directly to the quality of programmes developed for accreditation. Secondly, there is its contribution to a wider culture of effectiveness in the prison and probation services, where programme staff viewed the Panel's decisions in a mainly positive light, and expressed confidence in the programmes accredited by the Panel. In moving forward, the Panel should seek to build on these undoubted successes.

This is a time of development for the Panel, with major implications for its future relationship with the correctional services. As acknowledged at the Panel's full session on Friday 1 March 2002, 'What Works' is an evolving environment in England and Wales, and it is important for the Panel to remain at the forefront of these developments. The question raised is the direction in which JAP, now CSAP, might be moving given its new terms of reference, the adoption of the new integrated systems approach, revised programme accreditation criteria, and the imminent appointment of a new Panel. In considering this question, this final chapter, looks first at some structural issues that impinge on the legitimacy of the Panel, before reflecting on how its role might develop in the future. Rather than conclude with specific recommendations, as in earlier chapters, this chapter highlights a number of matters that the Panel might have on its agenda in developing its future role.

Structural issues and legitimacy

As has been seen, JAP is a non-departmental public body (NDPB), but one that is symbiotically linked to both the Prison Service and NPD. It differs radically from some other NDPBs – for example, the Youth Justice Board (YJB) has a sizeable budget for 'special initiatives', is in charge of purchase of services and of allocation practices in the juvenile secure estate, and has a significant role in monitoring the work of youth offending teams (YOTs). JAP's role is much more dependent on the relevant mainstream field agencies than is the YJB, and a significant element of its work is necessarily reactive, that is, waiting for appropriate applications to come forward for accreditation or advice. Despite this, JAP also wields significant power – programme developers can sometimes be devastated by, or very angry at, rejections (though these reactions are not usual), and JAP is widely seen in the field as controlling the kinds of treatment programme that are deemed acceptable. Thus, overall, JAP walks a tightrope between power over and dependence upon its linked fieldwork services. It is vital for its future development that the Panel develops this role sensitively.

Inevitably, the primary role of strategy development must lie with the prison and probation services, and JAP would not want to contest this. It has been noted, however, that JAP is also keen to play a developmental role where it perceives that the relevant field agency is having difficulty in developing accreditable programmes in a particular field of work. Where JAP sees a need for such a developmental role, it is typically more proactive, e.g. by being more willing to do site visits, provide extensive feedback, etc. That makes excellent policy sense, though it is also important that such activities are not seen as unduly favouring particular programmes, and therefore unfairly helping them by comparison with others. (See further below.)

As regards actual submissions to the Panel, there is now a well-established 'gatekeeper' system in both main agencies. Since the 'gatekeepers' regularly attend Panel meetings, however, the distinction between the Panel and the agencies (and their 'gatekeepers') sometimes looks very blurred from the field. There seems to be significant merit in keeping these roles clearly separate, so that the gatekeeper may advise, but decisions are clearly those of the Panel.

The existence of 'gatekeepers' has undoubtedly been, on balance, beneficial – both to the agencies (more professional programme development) and to JAP (fewer poor applications, therefore more efficient use of its limited time). Potentially, however, gatekeepers could stifle innovation – for example, if a probation board has a new programme which it regards as promising, but cannot gain access to JAP except through the NPD gatekeeper, who might be hostile to that kind of programme. Possibly this potential difficulty could be overcome by allowing some kind of appeal mechanism from gatekeepers to JAP in such circumstances.

Audit is another area where structural issues are raised. As more programmes become accredited, and fewer new programmes come forward for accreditation, the audit role will become increasingly important (as will the review of accredited programmes – see below). JAP itself cannot perform the main audit role (and none of the respondents suggested that it should), but it is essential that it retains some oversight over audit arrangements in the two services, or else these could drift into autonomous practices. JAP's clear awareness of the current differences between prison and probation audit systems, and its call for a move towards a more effective joint approach between the services, suggests it is already very alert to the importance of these matters. Indeed, JAP perhaps has a wider strategic role to play in promoting joint work between the prison and probation services, for example in the area of integrated throughcare systems (which are potentially of great importance as JAP moves into the 'whole systems' approach).

As the above comments suggest, JAP's interface with its two linked services in part demands sensitive attention to structural issues. In addition, however, issues of legitimacy are frequently raised – for example, by programme developers (who, for optimum future development, need to believe that the Panel operates with both professional competence and fairness) and programme staff (who sometimes confuse the Panel with their Service Headquarters). The way forward here seems to be for the Panel to emphasise its independence from (as well as its close working links with) the relevant services, and also to pay close attention to the research literature on fairness and legitimacy. Above all, that literature emphasises issues of *procedural justice* in promoting perceptions of legitimacy among those over whom a given body has power (see Tyler, 1990; Tyler and Blader, 2000). The elements of procedural justice that are seen as important by most subjects have been summarised in a number of research publications; the following (taken from Paternoster *et al.* 1997) is a representative list:

(i) *Participation/representation* The opportunity adequately to put one's case to decision maker(s) before a judgement is made by him/her/them.

(ii) *Dignity and respect* Being treated by the authorities as a human being, with rights, feelings, and status.

(iii) *Neutrality* The authority being willing and able to exercise an appropriate degree of neutrality and independence in handling the case.

(iv) *Competence* The authority appearing to be able to make high-quality decisions, and to explain them.

(v) *Consistency* The authority not acting arbitrarily, and, if different cases are judged differently, being able to explain why this is so.

(vi) *Correctability* The opportunity for initially unfair judgements to be corrected (for example, on appeal).

JAP generally seems to score reasonably well with programme staff on most of these criteria, but there also appears to be room for improvement.[19] In particular, the Panel could perhaps usefully review its practices in the light of the procedural justice literature, for example on conflict of interest issues (see under 'neutrality' above) and on issues of 'participation/representation' (where applicants did not always believe that Panel members had thoroughly absorbed submission documents, see Chapter 4).

The above remarks focus on the relationship between JAP and the prison and probation services. It should not be forgotten, however, that private sector providers (e.g. contracted-out prisons) may also apply to JAP without going through the prison/probation 'gatekeepers'. Potentially, this could lead to premature applications from such sources coming before the full Panel, and there have already been examples of this. Where this occurs, it is not an efficient use of the Panel's resources, and some filtering mechanism perhaps needs to be put in place, while retaining fairness and parity of treatment. This could be particularly relevant since, as indicated in the White Paper *Justice for All* (2002), the new plans for intermittent custody (now contained in the Criminal Justice Bill 2003) are intended to have both a strong offender behaviour programme focus and the possibility of 'imaginative options' for 'community custody centres' on prison sites (pages 94 and 113). If 'imaginative options' means an increasing role for the private sector, this issue could be of considerable importance for the Panel in the medium term.

The future role of the Panel

Panel members and policy advisers were clearly aware of the Panel's developing role, and readily discussed the implications of this. Some interviewees pointed to a need for JAP to move beyond considering individual applications to provide greater input into policy and strategic questions relating to programme development. It was argued that the Panel could draw on its considerable collective experience in the correctional field to contribute more broadly to curriculum development and decisions about piloting new approaches, for example by recommending new applications for techniques developed in accredited programmes. Perceiving a shift in focus from the production of new programmes to ensuring effective delivery and reviewing programmes, some argued that the Panel might have a role in helping to devise an action plan to improve the implementation and delivery of programmes in the light of findings from pathfinder projects. This point touches on the Panel's role in setting audit procedures and its relationship with the prison and probation services, as discussed above.

---

19 Although only 39 members of programme staff were aware of advice being given by the Panel, less than half rated that advice as very/quite useful or fair (see Appendix II).

A key area for likely future development is the Panel's role in reviewing programmes in the light of feedback from practitioners, and of audit and evaluation findings. In time, this will inevitably lead to questions such as whether to withdraw a particular accreditation, or to approve changes in design and content. The change control system designed by the Probation Service will provide a structure for this work. It remains to be seen whether this mechanism will achieve a proper balance between allowing the Panel to learn directly from practitioners (via regional 'What Works' managers, NPD and the Change Control Panel) and ensuring reasonable stability and certainty in programme content. Another test will come when the Panel examines the possible implications of evaluations of accredited programmes, such as the Oxford Probation Studies Unit's of Think First (see footnotes 5 and 16 above).

One question debated during the February/March 2002 meeting of the Panel was whether it should move into the accreditation of integrated systems, such as community punishment, case management and resettlement. This is a step it has now taken with the inclusion of integrated systems in its new terms of reference and the grant of Recognised Status to Enhanced Community Punishment in September 2002. There are interesting parallels here with the change in focus of health care accreditation from individual facilities to the connecting networks as it became clear that problems were more likely to arise during transitions between, for example, hospital and rehabilitation centre than in the hospital itself (Scrivens, 1995). Some JAP members expressed considerable enthusiasm for this kind of development, which they saw as a logical extension of their work, responding, for example, to the need to provide continuity of services. Others doubted the susceptibility of these broader approaches to the accreditation process, arguing that the Panel should stick to its 'core business' or a cognitive-behavioural focus rather than over-stretch itself by attempting to accredit everything. The following dangers were perceived in the Panel's adopting too wide a role in accrediting prison or probation activities: bureaucratic costs, diluting treatment programmes, and creating confusion over what exactly was being accredited.

These issues bear directly on the Panel's relationship with the prison and probation services, and its responsibility for assisting cultural change to effective practice in the two agencies. The new terms of reference approved for the Panel put greater emphasis on its collaboration with these correctional services (and possibly in future the Youth Justice Services), and its assistance with the implementation of 'What Works' through appropriate dialogue and communication. Of particular importance here is its promoting joint working between the Services to provide continuity in the interventions delivered to offenders in custody or the community, especially in view of proposals in the Criminal Justice Bill for Custody Plus and Intermittent Custody.

One important question for the future is how to maintain clear boundaries between the responsibilities of the Panel and those of its sponsoring bodies, while also ensuring that the Panel's resources are used most effectively to enable the prison and probation services to equip themselves with interventions that will reduce offending. On this point, interviews revealed an awareness that accreditation was not the only mechanism by which to promote good practice, but also some uncertainty as to where accreditation might sit alongside a range of other quality assurance measures operating internally within the correctional services, or applied by other bodies such as Inspectorates. During the period of the evaluation, an attempt to clarify this matter was being made by the Prison Service through developing a quality assurance framework for regime interventions, and it is a question that the correctional services will wish to continue to address in conjunction with the Panel. It seems important for the continued credibility of the Panel that it is seen to operate within a clearly defined sphere of activity requiring its particular expertise in research on, and the development and delivery of, interventions designed to reduce offending.

Thus, overall, the Panel can claim significant achievements since its creation; and in view of recent changes, it also faces significant new challenges for the future as it moves into new territory such as integrated systems, and its focus shifts from accrediting programmes towards reviewing them in the light of audit and evaluation findings and practitioner feedback. One purpose of this report has been to assist the Panel, and relevant policymakers, to move forward to face these new challenges in the light of a process-based assessment of the Panel's internal procedures, and of how its work is viewed by relevant stakeholders (including those in the correctional services charged with taking forward the 'What Works' agenda on a day-to-day basis). It is hoped that the findings presented in this report, and the accompanying recommendations, will make some contribution to the developing work of the Panel.

Appendix I Joint Accreditation Panel: Composition, Terms of Reference and Accreditation Criteria[20]

Membership

Chair: *Sir Duncan Nichol,* non-executive director of the Correctional Services Strategy Board and former Chief Executive of the National Health Service in England.

Appointed Members

Mrs Hilary Eldridge, Director, Lucy Faithfull Foundation.

Dr Dawn Fisher, Consultant Forensic Clinical Psychologist, Llanarth Court Psychiatric Hospital.

Prof. Don Grubin, Professor of Forensic Psychiatry, University of Newcastle upon Tyne/Newcastle City Health Trust.

Dr Moira Hamlin, formerly Head of Psychology Services, United Bristol NHS Trust.

Dr Norman Hoffmann, Senior Adviser, Abt Associates Inc., Cambridge, Massachusetts.

Dr Doug Lipton, Retired Senior Research Fellow, National Development and Research Institutes Inc., New York.

Prof. Mike Maguire, Professor of Criminology and Criminal Justice, Cardiff University.

Dr Janice Marques, Chief of Programme Development and Evaluation, California Dept. of Mental Health.

Dr William Murphy, Professor of Psychiatry, University of Tennessee.

Dr Frank Porporino, Senior Partner, T3 Associates Training and Consulting, Ottawa, Ontario.

Prof. Peter Raynor, Professor of Applied Social Studies, University of Wales, Swansea.

Mr Simon Shepherd, Forensic Psychologist and Chief Executive of the European Association for the Treatment of Addiction.

20 As at the time of the February/March 2002 Panel meeting.

Nominated Members

Mr Peter Atkinson, Governor of HM Prison Acklington.

Ms Elizabeth Barnard, Prison Service, Head of What Works Unit.

Mr Danny Clark, National Probation Directorate, Programme Development Manager.

Mr Chris Lewis, Home Office, Head of Offenders and Corrections Unit, Research, Development and Statistics Directorate.

Prof. Rod Morgan, HM Chief Inspector of Probation.

Mr David Perry, National Probation Directorate, Head of Implementation.

Mr Andrew Underdown, Assistant Chief Probation Board Officer, Greater Manchester.

Terms of Reference

- Recommending and annually reviewing accreditation criteria for programme design and delivery (approved by Home Secretary). Accrediting individual programme design;

- Authorising procedures for audit of programme delivery, and authorising an annual assessment of quality of actual delivery for Key Performance Indicator purposes for both Prison and Probation Services;

- Advising on curriculum development, and advising on related matters especially in relation to assessment of risk and need; and

- Assisting cultural change to effective practice in the Prison and Probation Services.

Accreditation Criteria (Summary)

1. A clear model of change backed by research evidence (i.e. the programme has a realistic evidence-based plan for creating change in offenders' future behaviour)

2. Selection of offenders (i.e. the programme chooses participants who need to change and whose risk is likely to be reduced by the programme)

3. Targeting dynamic risk factors (i.e. the programme chooses the areas of risk which need to be and can be offered)

4. Range of targets (i.e. chooses a range of risk areas to focus upon)

5. Effective methods (i.e. uses those proven to work)

6. Skills orientated (i.e. teaches skills for offence-free living)

7. Sequencing, intensity and duration (i.e. timetables for maximum impact in reducing risk)

8. Engagement and motivation (i.e. encourages a positive response)

9. Continuity of programmes and services (i.e. co-ordinates them to maximise the effect of treatment and monitoring)

10. Ongoing monitoring (i.e. checks the programme in action)

11. Ongoing evaluation (i.e. checks and develops what works)

Appendix II

Programme Staff Survey

Responses: Sent 254
  Received 167

Table 1: *Responses by area and job role*

Area (No. administered)	Tutors	Line Managers	Strategic Managers	Total (% administered)
Greater Manchester (55)***	20 (39)	6 (9)	3 (4)	29 (55%)
HMP Manchester (10)	4 (6)	4 (3)	1 (1)	9 (90%)
West Mercia (27)	12 (21)	4 (4)	2 (2)	18 (67%)
HMP Drake Hall (7)	2 (3)	1 (2)	2 (2)	5 (71%)
Nottinghamshire* (20)	7	4	1	12 (60%)
HMP Whatton (25)	9 (18)	3 (3)	3 (4)	15 (60%)
HMP Wellingborough (6)	3 (4)	1 (1)	0 (1)	4 (67%)
Thames Valley* (32)	11	3	3	17 (53%)
HMP Albany (25)	11 (20)	2 (2)	3 (3)	16 (64%)
HMP Full Sutton (33)	13 (21)	9 (9)	3 (3)	25 (76%)
Cambridgeshire (19)	8 (10)	1 (4)	5 (5)	14 (74%)
Total (254)	100	38	26	164 (66%) **

*   No data available for number sent by job role.
**   This figure does not include three responses received from Team Support Officers who do not fit into any of the above categories.
*** Of the total number sent in the Greater Manchester Region, three were sent to Team Support Officers, the total received from the area was therefore 32 (58%).

Demographic Characteristics of Sample

Gender: Male   70 (43%)

Female   92 (57%)

(missing cases 5)

Age: Evenly distributed in age groups between 20 and 60 years.
Only 2 people were under 20 and 2 people over 60.

Ethnicity: Sample is predominantly white (98%), with one representative from each of the groups Indian/Pakistani and Black Other, and two people in the Black Caribbean group. (Data on ethnicity is missing for only one respondent).

Work-related Characteristics of Sample

The sample has been divided into three groups for the purpose of analysis:

1. **Tutors (61%)** – involved in delivery of programmes (generally, Probation Service Assistant, Probation Officer, Prison Officer, Psychological Assistant, Psychologist)

2. **Line Managers (23%)** – manage tutors, manage particular aspects of programmes, and also deliver programmes, e.g. treatment managers or throughcare managers. (generally, Probation Officer, Higher Psychologist)

3. **Strategic Managers (16%)** – have a more strategic role, not involved in delivery, generally have management responsibilities for more than one programme, e.g. Programme Manager, Throughcare Manager (in respect of all programmes at a particular establishment), Accredited Programmes Implementation Manager, Director of Psychology, Head of Operations, Director of Resettlement, Head of Communications and Standards. (SPO, Higher Psychologist and above).

Length of Service

- Most respondents (79%) had been working on programmes for less than 6 years.

- Broadly speaking, tutors had worked on programmes for the shortest length of time, followed by line managers, and then strategic managers.

- 32% of tutors had worked on programmes for less than one year, 53% had worked on them for 1-5 years, only 15% had worked on programmes for more than 5 years.

- 70% of Line Managers had worked on programmes for 1-5 years, 8% for than less than one year and 22% for more than 5 years.

- As shown in Figure 1, the length of time that Strategic Managers had worked on programmes was less concentrated in one category. However, 80% had worked on them for ten years or less.

Figure 1: **Length of time on programmes**

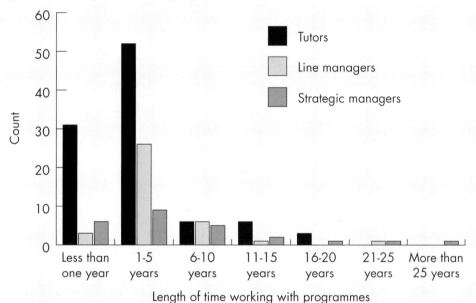

Length of time working with programmes

- The length of time worked in the Prison or Probation Service was fairly evenly distributed, although there was a larger number in the 1-5 years service category (34%) than in any of the others.
- 32 per cent of Strategic Managers had been working in the service more than 25 years; 8 of the 12 people who had worked in the service for over 25 years were Strategic Managers
- 88 per cent of tutors had been in the service for less than 16 years.
- There was a fairly even distribution of time served in the Line Manager group, although none had worked for less than 1 year, and only one for more than 25 years; 39 per cent of line managers fell into the 1-5 years service group.

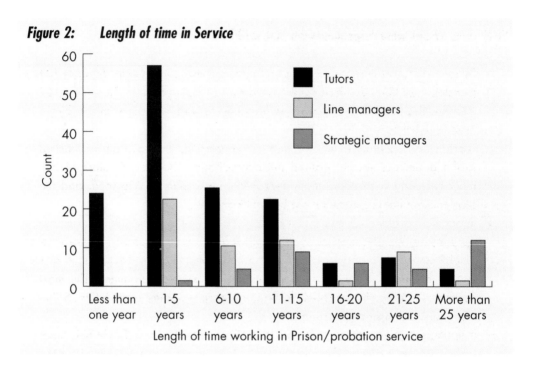

Figure 2:   Length of time in Service

Previous Experience

In answer to the question on work experience prior to working with programmes, broadly speaking:

- Tutors cited experience outside the Prison/Probation Services, such as teaching, youth work, experience in the armed forces or police and relevant educational qualifications, as well as general experience in the Prison or Probation Service.
- Line Managers cited relevant experience in the Services. They pointed to general experience with offenders, other Prison/Probation roles and experience delivering programmes.
- Strategic Managers pointed to other management experience within the Prison/Probation Service, other roles within the Services, and work with offenders.

Which programmes were respondents working with?

- By far the most well represented programmes were *Enhanced Thinking Skills* (34 people), *Sex Offender Treatment Programme* (46 people) and *Think First* (62 people). The accredited programmes respondents were working with are shown in Table 2 below.
- There were also practitioners working on programmes that have been submitted to the panel but not yet gained full accreditation; in total, 6 tutors, 4 line managers and 5 strategic managers mentioned Focus on Violence, and the substance misuse programmes ASRO and PRISM.
- In addition, respondents mentioned programmes not yet submitted to the panel, or developed locally such as domestic violence programmes, courses on employment, anger management and for women. In total, 14 tutors, 6 line managers and 8 strategic managers mentioned such programmes. The most common were locally produced domestic violence programmes (9 tutors, 5 line managers, and 4 strategic managers).
- It appears that training for *ETS, SOTP, R&R, One-to-One and CALM* had been undertaken by a greater number of people than were currently working on those programmes. It is unclear from the questionnaires why this is the case, but that data may indicate that respondents had been involved in these programmes in the past and were no longer working on them, or had recently been trained but had not yet run a course.
- It also appears that there are a number of people working on programmes that they have not been trained for. The figures indicate that this is the case for *Think First, Drink Impaired Drivers, ART,* and *Cognitive Self Change.* It is possible, however, that individuals did not specify all the training courses they had attended. (A few answered 'various' or 'numerous' in response to the question concerning training.) In addition, strategic managers often appear to manage programmes without having attended the basic training for them.
- Other training courses attended by tutors included motivational interviewing, psychometrics, general group work courses, and courses on particular offender groups such as violent offenders, sex offenders, or those with drug/alcohol issues.
- Line Managers had attended courses on assessment, supervision skills and treatment management.
- Strategic managers had also received training on treatment management, throughcare management, programme management, and audit training.
- Several respondents from each group had attended domestic violence training.

Table 2: Experience of programmes

Programme	Number working on each programme			Total	Number who have received training			Total
	Tutors	Line M'gers	Strategic M'gers		Tutors	Line M'gers	Strategic M'gers	
ETS[1]	18	8	8	34	23	9	7	39
SOTP[2]	28	9	9	46	32	11	9	52
R&R[3]	6	3	2	11	7	3	2	12
CSOGP[4]	6	2	5	13	5	3	3	11
Think First	42	11	9	62	38	13	7	58
One-to-One	8	3	4	15	10	2	4	16
Drink-impaired Drivers	8	5	5	18	5	5	2	12
ART[5]	6	2	3	11	5	1	1	7
Cognitive Self Change	1	3	2	6	1	3	0	4
CALM[6]	1	0	0	1	3	1	0	4

1 Enhanced Thinking Skills
2 Sex Offender Treatment Programme (Core, Adapted, Rolling, Booster)
3 Reasoning and Rehabilitation
4 Community Sex Offender Group-work Programme
5 Aggression Replacement Training
6 Coping with Anger and Learning to Manage it

What Works

The majority of respondents (83.8%) felt that they had a 'reasonable overview' or 'some knowledge' of the 'What Works' research. Figure 3 below shows this in relation to the three job role categories identified earlier. The distribution of knowledge in the two management groups shows that, as groups, they have slightly more knowledge than the tutors. Only individuals in the 'tutor' category admitted to having no knowledge of the literature.

Figure 3: *Knowledge of What Works Research*

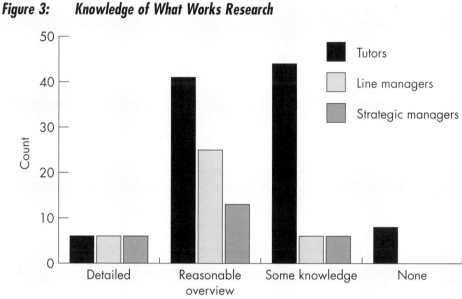

Knowledge of research on offender programmes

There was overwhelming agreement with the emphasis on programme design being aimed at reducing offending:

- 46 per cent 'strongly agreed' with this emphasis and 50 per cent 'agreed'.
- This pattern was the case irrespective of management/tutor role. Only 7 tutors out of the whole sample had a neutral attitude towards the issue; those who were interviewed confirmed that they had answered 'neutral' to those questions about which they lacked sufficient information to comment. No one had a negative attitude. This is shown below in Figure 4.

Figure 4: Agreement with focus on Reoffending

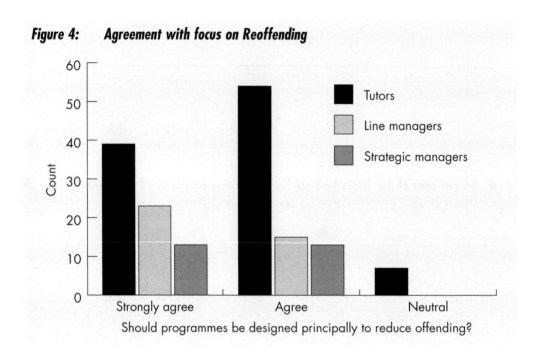

Should programmes be designed principally to reduce offending?

Many (64.8%) agreed that reconviction rates serve as a reasonable measure of programme effectiveness. However, there was little strong agreement (2.5%) and a number of respondents neither agreed nor disagreed (21%), or disagreed (14.2%).

By job role, the figures are as follows:

- Tutors:

Strongly Agree	2%
Agree	60%
Neutral	26%
Disagree	12%

- Line Managers

Strongly Agree	3%
Agree	55%
Neutral	16%
Disagree	26%

- Strategic Managers

Strongly Agree	4%
Agree	81%
Neutral	12%
Disagree	4%

JAP

- 81 per cent of the sample had heard of JAP, and 55 per cent had heard of earlier panels.

- All of the Strategic Managers and 70 per cent of the Tutors had heard of JAP, only one Line Manager had not.

- 56 per cent of the Tutors had not heard of other panels but 61 per cent of Line Managers and 88 per cent of the Strategic Managers had.

The sources of information about JAP and other panels are shown in Tables 3 and 4 (below). Of those in all three staff groups who had heard of either JAP or earlier panels, colleagues were the most common source of information. It was also common for those in all groups to get information from managers. It appears that both Line and Strategic Managers are more likely to obtain information on JAP from training than are Tutors, and that Strategic Managers are much more likely to use conference presentations, professional journals and Probation Circulars as sources of information than the other groups.

Table 3: Information about Panel

Source of Information	% of sample	% of those who had heard of JAP or earlier panels
Colleagues	59%	68%
Managers	47%	54%
Training	40%	46%
Conference presentations	24%	28%
Professional journals	21%	24%
Probation Circulars	21%	24%
Internet	1%	1%

Table 4: Information about Panel by job role

Source of Information	% of Tutors who had heard of Panels	% of Line Managers	% of Strategic Managers
Colleagues	70%	65%	65%
Managers	51%	57%	62%
Training	38%	54%	58%
Conference presentations	14%	35%	62%
Professional journals	19%	24%	42%
Probation Circulars	22%	8%	54%
Internet	1%	0%	4%

Sources of information cited under 'other' were as follows: personal contact with JAP; OBPU managers meetings; involved in a submission to JAP; JAP annual report; Prison Service; family; researchers; and 'part of own job'.

JAP's Role

The way in which JAP's role was perceived by those who had heard of JAP, in relation to their practice, fell into 8 themes as follows:

- Overseer (31%)

This category included comments relating to overseeing programmes, determining which programmes are used, accrediting programmes, determining criteria to be applied to programmes, and considering submissions from new programmes.

- Quality Control (41%)

This category included comments that pointed to the maintenance of standards, audit, evaluation of programme quality, and monitoring.

- Design (13%)

Comments relating to the ongoing development of programmes, and advising on content and delivery.

- Research (5%)

Included identifying what is effective and useful, assessing the potential and success of programmes, and advising on ongoing research.

- Interface (2%)

Comments that pointed to JAP acting as a nexus between the Prison and Probation Services, and the development of programmes that can be used in both.

- Distant / Unconnected to Practice (8%)

JAP feels disconnected from day to day work.

- Equal Opportunities (0.7%)

Providing equal access to programmes for all offenders and equality across the country.

- Unclear / Don't Know (9%)

Role of JAP is unclear.

Table 5 relates the above to job role.

Table 5: Role of Panel

Perception of JAP's role	% of Tutors who had heard of JAP	% of Line Managers	% of Strategic Managers
Overseer	27%	32%	38%
Quality Control	31%	59%	46%
Design	9%	22%	12%
Research	2%	3%	15%
Interface	2%	0%	4%
Distant/Unconnected	9%	14%	0%
Equal Opportunities	1%	0%	0%
Unclear/Don't know	14%	3%	4%

It is interesting to note that the Strategic Managers, who possess the most detailed information about JAP, and who do not have a 'hands on' role in programme delivery, did not feel that JAP was distant or unconnected to their practice.

Knowledge of JAP's decisions

Responses about knowledge of JAP's decisions so far were varied. Tutors mostly had only a small amount of knowledge (40%) or none at all (49%). Amount of knowledge appears to increase with seniority, 58 per cent of Strategic Managers having a reasonable overview or detailed knowledge, and 34 per cent of Line Managers having a reasonable overview (Figure 5).

Figure 5:   *Knowledge of Panel decisions*

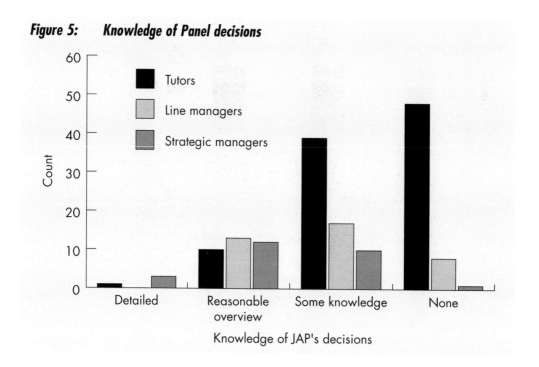

Knowledge of JAP's decisions

There was a largely positive reaction to JAP's decisions so far, only 6 people rating their decisions as poor or very poor. A large proportion of the sample (46%), however, gave the answer 'neutral' and 26 per cent did not answer the question. Those who knew least about JAP's decisions were more likely to register neutral views, as were tutors (Figures 6 and 7).

Figure 6: *Views of Panel decisions by amount of knowledge*

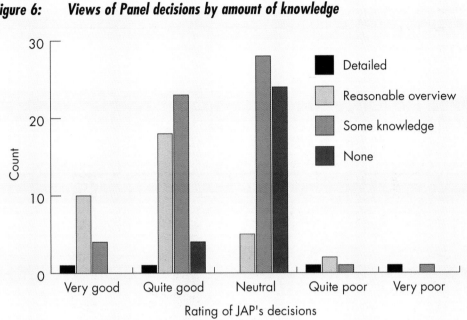

Figure 7: *Views of Panel decisions by job role*

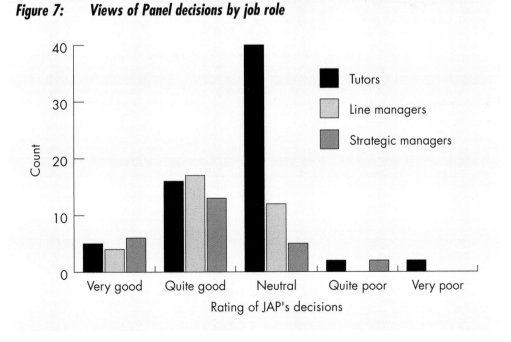

Knowledge of accreditation criteria

The manager groups appeared to have more knowledge than the tutors (49% of tutors had no knowledge of the criteria) as shown below. In total, 63 per cent of the sample had some degree of knowledge, 33 per cent had no knowledge, and 5 per cent did not answer.

Figure 8: Knowledge of Accreditation Criteria by job role

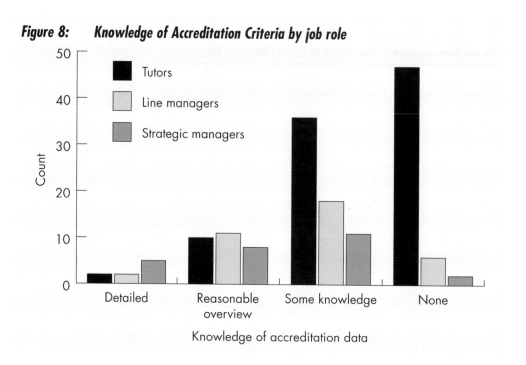

In registering their views on the accreditation criteria, the only statement with which more agreed than disagreed was that the criteria set high standards that increase the likelihood of effectiveness. Full results are shown in Table 6, percentage figures relate to the percentage of the total number who answered the question (n=120). Only 47 people did not answer the question, whereas 55 claimed in the earlier question not to have any knowledge of the criteria. It must therefore be assumed that either some of those with no knowledge answered this question, or some of the non-respondents to the earlier question answered this one.

Table 6: *Views of Accreditation Criteria*

Statement relating to accreditation criteria	'Yes'	'No'
Set high standards that increase the likelihood of effectiveness	79%	21%
Set unreasonable expectations	14%	86%
Are about right in improving the quality of programmes	39%	61%
Are too vague in specifying what is required	6%	94%
Set standards that can be applied to all offenders	24%	76%
Do not take account of the needs of some offenders (diversity)	40%	60%

Thirty-three people took the opportunity to make additional comments about the accreditation criteria. Three themes came out of these comments as follows:

- **Diversity** – mentioned by 10 people. Concern exists over the cultural specificity of some programmes and a concentration on male offenders. Respondents were concerned that programmes are unable to meet the different needs of the following offender groups: ethnic minorities, women, those with learning difficulties or low IQ scores, disabled and hearing impaired individuals.
- **Flexibility** – mentioned by 6 people. Accredited programmes were regarded as inflexible and therefore unresponsive to individual circumstances or groups. The theoretical principles regarded as effective are not flexibly applied, and alternative approaches are not considered. The requirement for programmes to be accredited was also regarded by one individual as restricting the number of programmes available to be used with offenders in order to address diverse needs.
- **Context of delivery** – mentioned by 5 people. The accreditation process was regarded by these individuals as insensitive to differences in the context of delivery, resources and time available.

JAP's Advice

Thirty-nine people were aware of advice given by JAP on a programme on which they were working. Managers appeared to be more aware of advice that was given – 15 per cent of Tutors were aware of advice, 36 per cent of Line Managers and 41 per cent of Strategic Managers. The percentage of the sample from each area aware of advice from JAP is shown in Table 7 (below).

Table 7: Received Panel's Advice

Site	% aware of advice from JAP
Probation:	
Greater Manchester	10%
West Mercia	28%
Nottinghamshire	8%
Thames Valley	29%
Cambridgeshire	21%
Prison:	
HMP Manchester	22%
HMP Drake Hall	20%
HMP Whatton	27%
HMP Wellingborough	25%
HMP Albany	31%
HMP Full Sutton	36%

Those who were aware of advice rated it as follows:

Very useful	13%	Very fair	10%
Quite useful	36%	Quite fair	36%
Middling	26%	Middling	31%
Of little use	15%	Quite unfair	5%
Of no use	3%	Very unfair	5%
Missing data	7%	Missing data	13%

Audit

Most respondents (94% of those who answered the question) had at least some knowledge of audit procedures. Managers had more knowledge than tutors – 46 per cent of Line Managers and 50 per cent of Strategic Managers had detailed knowledge of audit procedures compared to only 3 per cent of Tutors.

Figure 9: Knowledge of Audit

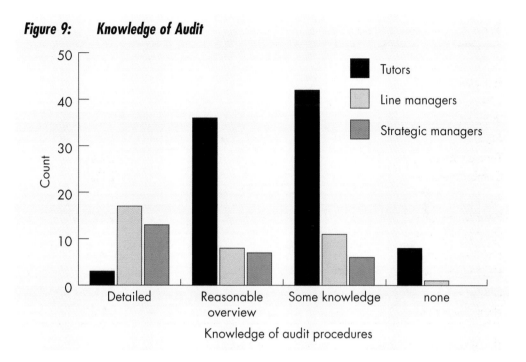

- 62.5% said that a programme they were working on had been audited.
- Those working in prisons were either slightly more aware of being audited, or had been audited on a greater number of occasions. Only in West Mercia and Cambridgeshire did the 'no' responses outnumber the 'yes's (Table 8 overleaf).
- Where people were aware of being audited, they predominantly regarded the audits as fair and useful as shown in Figure 10 (overleaf).

Table 8:   Experience of Audit

Site	Audited?			Total
	Yes	No	Unsure	
Probation:				
Gtr Manchester	18	12	0	30
West Mercia	3	15	0	18
Nottinghamshire	11	1	0	12
Thames Valley	12	5	0	17
Cambridgeshire	1	11	1	13
Prison:				
HMP Manchester	6	3	0	9
HMP Drake Hall	5	0	0	5
HMP Whatton	14	0	0	14
HMP Wellingborough	2	1	0	3
HMP Albany	13	2	0	15
HMP Full Sutton	23	2	0	25
Total	108	52	1	161 *

*   6 responses are missing

Figure 10:   Audit Useful?

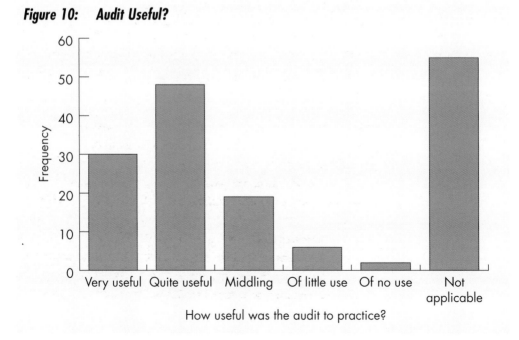

How useful was the audit to practice?

Figure 11: Audit Fair?

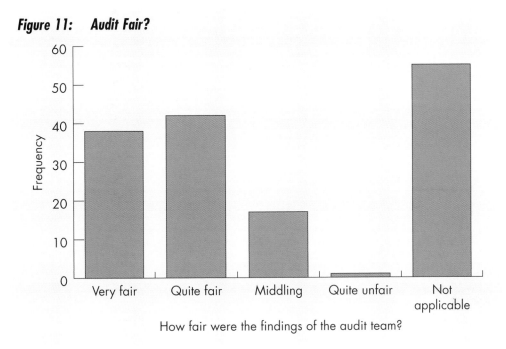

How fair were the findings of the audit team?

Analysis by Prison/Probation

The analysis of the above issues according to whether respondents were working in a prison or a probation area shows that more prison staff had heard about JAP. Prison staff also had more knowledge of JAP's decisions, rated them more highly, and appeared to view audit findings more positively. Attitudes to JAP's advice were no different as between workplace.

Table 9: Comparing Prison and Probation Views

		Prisons		Probation
Heard of JAP?		89%		72%
Knowledge of JAP's decisions	0%	detailed	4%	detailed
	32%	reasonable overview	13%	reasonable overview
	40%	some knowledge	40%	some knowledge
	28%	none	43%	none
Rating of JAP's decisions	15%	very good	9%	very good
	47%	quite good	27%	quite good
	36%	neutral	57%	neutral
	2%	quite poor	4%	quite poor
	0%	very poor	3%	very poor
Rating of audit findings	47%	very fair	26%	very fair
	42%	quite fair	44%	quite fair
	10%	middling	28%	middling
	0%	quite unfair	3%	quite unfair
	0%	very unfair	0%	very unfair
Rating of JAP's advice	15%	very fair	7%	very fair
	40%	quite fair	43%	quite fair
	35%	middling	36%	middling
	5%	quite unfair	7%	quite unfair
	5%	very unfair	7%	very unfair

Appendix III   JAP's Accredited Programmes: Showing Progress Towards Accreditation

A. General Offending Behaviour Programmes

Programme Advice? Formal application

Cognitive   No
Self
Change
(CSCP)

Recognised March 2000
- **Model of change:** adding contextual and situational factors would help staff understand high-risk situations for offenders.
- **Selection of offenders:** should record assessment of neuro-psychological conditions by appropriately qualified person. Criteria would select large numbers of violent offenders, but number of places available limited. Additional assessment measures should be made explicit.
- **Range of targets:** should consider additional factors that could result in general rather than violent offending. More detail needed about referral re vocational factors, relationships and education.
- **Sequencing:** Block 6 inadequately developed/flexible, too short.
- **Engagement and motivation:** motivation needs more attention. Stronger emphasis needed on dealing with discriminatory comments/potentially volatile situations.
- **Continuity:** more detail needed on using family/friends to monitor behaviour, and required links to other agencies. Should specify arrangements to provide future supervisory probation staff.
- **Ongoing monitoring:** no audit criteria included. Ongoing evaluation: follow-up period should be increased, preferably to 2 years.

Accredited September 2000
- **Sequencing:** concern about developing and maintaining tutors skills for post-release module.
- **Engagement and motivation:** clarification needed about mandatory involvement of significant others in treatment. Practical demonstrations of the intention to defuse volatile situations, including those arising from race/culture, needed.
- **Continuity:** further submission required to sanction alteration of post-release arrangements for supervising officer and tutor to be same person. Further advice needed on linking relapse prevention plan and supervision plan within probation case record - also on programme management responsibilities given small numbers taking post-release module.
- **Ongoing evaluation:** evaluation of cost-effectiveness of post-release module suggested.

Programme	Advice?	Formal application

Enhanced Thinking Skills (ETS) — No

Accredited September 2000
- **Range of targets:** given relatively small range of targets directly addressed, clarity needed on case management role in addressing social risk factors presented by community as opposed to prison life.
- **Sequencing:** concern that limited in length, at lower end of acceptable dosage for medium/high risk offenders. Generic cognitive skills booster programmes should be used where available rather than post-programme sessions with case manager.
- **Engagement and motivation:** not clear whether low motivation excludes or addressed in pre-programme work. Insufficient attention to retention. Engagement/motivation should be covered in tutors training.
- **Continuity:** suggested post-programme work not appropriate, scoring provisional pending development of generic cognitive skills booster.
- **Ongoing monitoring:** National treatment manual needs to specify the competencies required by treatment managers to carry out the role of supervisor and quality controller. Two points awarded in the expectation that the programme will meet the requirements set by the revised manual.

One-to-One — March 2000

Recognised September 2000
- **Model of change:** greater discussion needed relating motivational theory to one-to-one work.
- **Selection:** inconsistencies remain on target risk group. Should consider including those with low initial motivation. Policy on potential participants with substance misuse problems where no PRISM programme should be made explicit.
- **Effective methods:** Insufficient training/practice in motivational interviewing and delivery.
- **Engagement and motivation:** Tutor training manual needs to be more user friendly with more skill-based practice guidance.
- **Continuity:** need to address how programme would tie in with supervision planning.
- **Ongoing monitoring:** required to maintain programme integrity.
- **Ongoing evaluation:** wide variations likely in type of offenders, access to programme, and local availability of other services e.g. PRISM. Should cover relationship between facilitator and offender – possibly critical in effectiveness.

One-to-One — March 2000

Accredited March 2001
- **Selection of offenders:** no response made to previous recommendation to consider including those with low initial motivation
- **Effective methods/engagement and motivation:** accreditation will be suspended in absence of national training programme in motivational interviewing within one year. Tutor training manuals still stilted and dense.
- **Continuity:** managers' one day training should be revised to focus more specifically on how management task relates to programme and its requirements – revised manual must be submitted for approval within 12 months.

Programme	Advice?	Formal application
Reasoning and Rehabilitation (RAR)	No	**Accredited September 2000** ● **Selection of offenders:** some scope for improving assessment of motivation – question whether appropriate to exclude for low-motivation in face of evidence that involvement in programme can increase motivation. Would be useful for documentation to clarify arrangements for meeting additional needs. ● **Engagement and motivation:** need to resolve possible contradictions in manuals on staff selection and training. Panel would welcome more detail on how high completion rates will be ensured. ● **Ongoing monitoring:** need to consider how to monitor completion of homework.
Think First (TF)	No	**Recognised November 1999** ● **Sequencing:** too many factors addressed in time available. Post programme sessions should be more clearly linked to core programme and reinforce its learning. ● **Selection of offenders:** insufficiently defined and inconsistent. ● **Engagement and participation:** demands relatively high level of literacy. Theoretical underpinnings are culturally neutral. Description of motivational interviewing (MI) techniques too simple – staff training should be addressed. Attendance and compliance rates need improvement. Summary of training needed.

Advice on resubmission document March 2000
● **Note:** development of generic cognitive booster programme will influence final design. Also rescheduling of sessions will be informed by results of retrospective evaluation. Programme thus incomplete and application not scored.
● **Sequencing:** reconviction study will help address previous concerns. Also needs evidence of effectiveness in addressing the range of targets. Concern about objectives in post-programme sessions - case managers might not be able to facilitate them with same clarity as course tutors.
● **Selection of offenders:** guidelines should give greater weight to probation officers' assessments of motivation if staff have completed MI training. Should emphasise further the need to discuss cases where motivation appears low. Additional guidance on assessing cognitive deficits needed so offenders are not wrongly excluded.
● **Engagement and participation:** Work still needed on whether programme runs equally well with women, black or Asian offenders and whether they suffer discrimination either within programme or in access/selection.
● **Other issues:** tutor selection – some improvements can be made to selection interview and process. Research needed on relationship between performance in assessment process, training, and delivery of programme. More information needed on pass/fail criteria for training course.

Accredited September 2000
● **Ongoing evaluation:** limited evidence of programme's effectiveness – evaluation report inconclusive. Panel welcomes provision of further information on measures used to assess offenders pre and post programme.

B. Sex Offender Programmes

Programme   Advice?   Formal application

**Sex
Offender
Treatment
(SOTP)**

**Nov
1999**

Accredited March 2000

- **Model of change:** focuses on problems arising in puberty, should also acknowledge that problems could arise at other times.
- **Selection of offenders:** criteria difficult to follow, e.g. on meaning of high denial, which risk assessment measure is being used, and how brain damage, mental illness and potential for self-harm assessed for exclusion criteria. Manual needs to specify training/monitoring required for those doing psychometric and PCL-R assessments, backed by audit criteria.
- **Range of targets:** audit criteria needed on whether those with deviant sexual interest go on to extended programme or behaviour therapy.
- **Effective methods:** Training and programme manuals need more detail.
- **Engagement and motivation:** audit criteria needed to measure numbers of staff attending training on working with black offenders. Fundamental skills training should cover cultural awareness/culturally sensitive situations.
- **General comments and recommendations:** Greater clarification could be given about 'old me', 'new me' and 'future me'. Glossary of terms, contents list/index would be useful. Panel regrets dropping of exercise on establishing a hierarchy of offences.

**SOTP
Rolling**

**Nov
1999**

Recognised 1) September 2000

- **Selection of offenders:** More work needed on exclusion criteria, e.g. some with mental illness may find it beneficial. Assessment should be done by clinicians who can judge offenders' readiness/ability to meet demands of programme.
- **Effective methods**: Would benefit from additional work on cognitive distortions that could be picked up in relapse prevention module. Needs work on modifying cognitive distortions. More guidance needed on use of personal examples. Treatment targets often over-ambitious.
- **Skills orientated:** Needs more opportunity to develop skills during role-play. Lack of guidance for tutors on learning objectives, outcomes sought, and how to achieve.
- **Ongoing monitoring:** audit criteria needed to ensure that programme should preceded by participation in a cognitive skills programme.
- **Training manual:** should state clear learning objectives. Fundamental skills training handbook would benefit from section on victimology. Should distinguish carefully between modelling and self-disclosure, and contain guidance on dealing with participants' disclosures.

Programme	Advice?	Formal application

SOTP Rolling — Nov 1999

Recognised 2) March 2001
- **Selection of offenders:** needs to cover brain damage and assessment of suitability by a psychiatrist.
- **Effective methods:** Section on cognitive distortions needs more realistic examples. Lacks work on modifying cognitive distortions. Treatment targets still over-ambitious. Need for guidance on use of personal examples not fully addressed.
- **Skills orientated:** More examples and instruction to tutors needed.
- **Training manual:** particularly high standard of tutor training needed – detailed training manual needed to ensure effective delivery.

Accredited October 2001
- **Effective methods:** need for psychiatric or psychological assessor to be familiar with programme has been overlooked.
- **Ongoing monitoring:** training manual should be updated as new research on effective delivery emerges.

SOTP Extended — No

Accredited March 2002
- **Selection of offenders:** should be requirement for assessment of those with mental illness or head injuries to be done by Psychiatrist familiar with programme content.
- **Skills orientated:** Fully met. Concern over difficulty of work on intimacy skills in the prison setting. Not clear what expected of offenders with regard to providing accounts of fantasy and deviant thoughts/behaviours in a group setting.
- **Sequencing:** monitoring required to ensure that between session work not too burdensome on top of 4 sessions a week.
- **Engagement:** focus on rapists and heterosexual relationships – should be broadened to include gay relationships and examples appropriate for child molesters.

Northumbria — March 2001

Accredited October 2001
- **Model of change:** motivation should be included in list of factors pertinent to change.
- **Selection of offenders:** handling of intra-familial offenders and sadistic offenders needs to be addressed.
- **Effective methods:** examples must address range of offenders and offending patterns.
- **Skills orientated:** insufficient time for practice of social functioning skills.
- **Sequencing:** suggest more flexibility in duration of exercises for offenders who need varying amounts of time to complete them.
- **Continuity:** needs guidelines on post-programme report and clearly specifying future services.
- **Additionally:** Awareness of approaches taken by SOTP needed for those going on to relapse prevention group.

Programme	Advice?	Formal application

Thames Valley — **Nov 1999** — **Accredited March 2001**
- **Selection of offenders:** should consider including offenders who need Project sign language assistance.
- **Targeting dynamic risk factors:** should clarify how concept of deviancy applies to rapists - classification used derives from child molesters research.
- **Range of targets:** section explaining fantasy modification should be removed – local areas will decide how to provide this work. Purpose/relevance of Life Skills programme should be explained more fully to offenders at start module.
- **Effective methods:** clear guidelines needed on when to include non-intimate partners in partners' programme. More guidance needed on victim letter writing. No mention of homosexual relationships in Life Skills programme. Recommendations on dealing constructively with jealousy needed, plus opportunity for review of homework on jealousy.
- **Sequencing:** all elements of programme may not be necessary for low-risk, low-deviancy, high-contextual risk offenders.
- **Engagement and Motivation:** Training manual for partners' programme incomplete. Some objectives phrased using negative language.

West Midlands — **March 2000** — **Accredited September 2000 (Limited accreditation of booster programme)**
- **Model of change:** concern that theory manual model has not been accurately applied.
- **Selection of offenders:** 12 months stabilisation on medication prior to programme for those with mental illness is excessive. Outside clinicians need adequate understanding of programmes to assess suitability. Policy on working with black offenders should be included in training and management manuals.
- **Range of targets:** Relatively little time spent on deviant sexual fantasy. Needs access to work on behaviour modification in relapse prevention plans. Some relapse prevention time needed on family contacts and possible family support for pro-offending attitudes (should be covered in training manual).
- **Effective methods:** Too many skills taught too quickly without enough time for practice. Use of Health Education staff to deliver sessions on sexual fantasy should be reconsidered. Should ensure those with most severe deficits are referred on for further sex education work. Training manual should prepare staff to manage emotional reactions of offenders and families. Teaching assertion through an alcohol related scenario should be avoided.
- **Continuity:** management and training manuals should show how the programme works with other agencies.

C. Other programmes

Programme   Advice? Formal application

Aggression   **1) Mar**   **Recognised March 2001**
Replacement   **2000**   ● **Selection of offenders:** ART selection matrix still needs work.
Training   **2) Sept** ● **Sequencing:** Lack of time to practise skills.
(ART)   **2000**   **Accredited October 2001**
  ● **Selection of offenders:** Programme not fully accredited for use with women
  – evaluation data required in one year.

Controlling   **No**   **Recognised March 2000**
Anger and   ● **Model of change:** Panel not convinced about evidence on effectiveness
Learning to   of anger management programmes.
Manage it   ● **Selection of offenders:** Not possible to identify offenders for whom anger
(CALM)   is a key dynamic risk factor.
  ● **Continuity:** Need to ensure terminology consistent with cog skills
  programmes. Needs clear throughcare strategy.
  ● **Ongoing evaluation:** Needed to assess whether programme effective,
  disentangling different treatments.

  Accredited September 2000
  ● **Selection of offenders:** Data to be provided to satisfy Panel that interview
  for selection de-selects unsuitable offenders.
  ● **Continuity:** Satisfactory pending development of generic booster
  programme with detailed outline of sessions and training plan.
  ● **Ongoing evaluation:** Panel would welcome 1 year reconviction data as
  well as 2 year outcomes. Methodology to distinguish effects of this
  programme from other programmes.

Drink   **March**   **Recognised September 2000**
Impaired   **2000**   ● **Effective methods:** Needs more integration and opportunity to acquire,
Drivers   practice, reinforce skills.
(DIDS)   ● **Sequencing:** similar points.
  ● **Engagement and motivation:** More training time for tutors required.
  Concern about non-start – needs attention to case management pre-
  programme and motivation.

  Accredited March 2001 (For use with male offenders)
  ● **Selection of offenders:** No additional materials/resources provided for
  female offenders.
  ● **Effective methods:** Inadequate opportunity to practice skills.
  ● **Skills orientated:** Lack of opportunity for reinforcement through practice.
  ● **Sequencing:** Intensity and duration not yet satisfactory.
  ● **Engagement and motivation:** Recommendation to give more attention to pre-
  programme motivation not addressed.
  ● **Ongoing evaluation:** Recommendation to establish system of data
  collection not addressed.

Programme	Advice?	Formal application
RAPt Substance Abuse	No	**Recognised November 1999**

Recognised November 1999

- **Model of change:** Insufficient evidence that 12 step programmes in prison work with anti-social drug dependent offenders. Also weak methods by which to identify offenders whose substance abuse is linked to other crime. Controlled reconviction study needed comparing starters with non-starters.
- **Effective methods:** Must be able to show that the 12 step method effective. Needs clearer specification of staff training. Methods used to prepare offenders for handling a lapse must be more explicit. Manuals need to cover HIV education.
- **Skills:** Skills component insufficiently specified.
- **Range of targets:** Programme intensively targets narrow but important dynamic risk factor, but not clear whether sufficient for this population.

Accredited September 2000

- Confidence that the programme is capable of reducing re-offending increased as a result of US research findings and additional data supplied on post programme drug use and reconviction.
- Previous concern about weak methods of identifying those whose criminality is demonstrably related to their substance abuse not yet resolved – selection procedures need to be clarified.
- An additional application needed to accredit programme for use with young offenders and in non-custodial settings.

References

Barbalet, J. M. (1998) *Emotion, Social Theory and Social Structure: A Macrosociological Approach*, Cambridge: Cambridge University Press.

Bernfeld, G. A., Farrington, D. P. and Leschied, A. W. (2001) *Offender Rehabilitation in Practice: Implementing and Evaluating Effective Programs*, Chichester: Wiley.

Bottoms, A. E., Gelsthorpe, L. R. and Rex, S. A. (2001) *Community Penalties: Change and Challenges*, Cullompton, Devon: Willan Publishing.

Crawford, A. (1998) *Crime Prevention and Community Safety*, London: Longman.

Friendship, C., Blud, L., Erikson, M. and Travers, R. (2002) An Evaluation of Cognitive Behavioural Treatment for Prisoners, *Research Finding 161*, London: Home Office.

Gelmon, *et al.* (1999) *Strategies for Change and Improvement*, San Francisco: University of California.

Gendreau, P., P. Smith and C. Goggin, (1999) "The Forgotten Issue in Effective Correctional Treatment: Program Implementation", *International Journal of Offender Therapy and Comparative Criminology* 43(2), 180-187.

Hollin, C., McGuire, J., Palmer, E., Bilby, C., Hatcher, R. and Holmes, A. (2002) Introducing Pathfinder Programmes into the Probation Service: An Interim Report, *Home Office Research Study No. 247*, London: Home Office.

Home Office (2002) *Justice For All*, Cm 5563, London, TSO.

Hope, T. and Murphy, D. J. (1983) "Problems of Implementing Crime Prevention: The Experience of a Demonstration Project", *Howard Journal*, 22, 38-50.

HM Prison Service (2001) *Annual Report and Accounts 2000/1*, London: HM Prison Service.

HM Prison Service (2002) *Annual Report and Accounts 2001/2*, London: HM Prison Service.

HMI Probation (2002) *Annual Report 2001/2*, London: Home Office.

Joint Prison/Probation Services Accreditation Panel (2001) *Annual Report 2000/1 – What Works: Towards Effective Practice*, http://www.homeoffice.gov.uk/cpd/probu.htm

Joint Prison/Probation Services Accreditation Panel, HMI Probation, and National Probation Service (2002) *Performance Standards Manual for the Delivery of Accredited Group Work Programmes*, London: Home Office.

McGuire, J. (1995) *What Works: Reducing Re-offending*, Chichester: Wiley Press.

McGuire, J. (2002) "Integrating Findings From Research Reviews", in J. McGuire (ed.) *Offender Rehabilitation and Treatment: Effective Programmes and Policies to Reduce Re-offending*, Chichester: Wiley Press.

National Probation Service (2001) *A New Choroegraphy: An Integrated Strategy for the National Probation Service for England and Wales*, London: Home Office.

Paternoster, R., Brame, R., Bachman, R. and Sherman, L. W. (1997) "Do Fair Procedures Matter? The Effect of Procedural Justice on Spouse Assault", *Law and Society Review*, 31, 163-204.

Pickering, E. (1996) "Evaluating the Benefits and Limitation of an Accreditation System", *World Hospital*, 31(1), 31-35.

Powis, B. and Walmsley, R. (2002) Programmes for Black and Asian Offenders on Probation: Lessons for Developing Practice, *Home Office Research Study No. 250*, London: Home Office.

Scrivens, E. (1995) *Accreditation: Protecting the Professional or the Consumer*, Buckingham: Open University Press.

Social Exclusion Unit (2002) *Reducing Re-offending by Ex-Prisoners*, London: Social Exclusion Unit.

Tyler,T. R. (1990) *Why People Obey the Law*, New Haven: Yale University Press.

Tyler, T. R. and Blader, S. L. (2000) *Co-operation in Groups: Procedural Justice, Social Identity and Behavioral Engagement*, Psychology Press.

Underdown, A (1998) *Strategies for Effective Offender Supervision*, Report of the HMIP What Works Project, London: Home Office.

Underdown, A. (2001) "Making "What Works work: challenges in the delivery of community penalties", in A. E. Bottoms, L. R. Gelsthorpe and S. A. Rex (eds.) *Community Penalties: Change and Challenges*, Cullompton, Devon: Willan Publishing.

Requests for Publications

Copies of our publications and a list of those currently available may be obtained from:

Home Office
Research, Development and Statistics Directorate
Communication Development Unit
Room 275, Home Office
50 Queen Anne's Gate
London SW1H 9AT
Telephone: 020 7273 2084 (answerphone outside of office hours)
Facsimile: 020 7222 0211
E-mail: publications.rds@homeoffice.gsi.gov.uk

alternatively

why not visit the RDS web-site at
          Internet: http://www.homeoffice.gov.uk/rds/index.htm

where many of our publications are available to be read on screen or downloaded for printing.